Conflict Resolution
A Foundation Guide

Susan Stewart has taught conflict resolution and mediation and been involved in the development of innovative university courses covering these topics. She has published extensively in the education field, including works on adult learning. In recent years she has been engaged in mediation as a teacher, researcher and community consultant.

D0540223

WITHDRAWN

Conflict Resolution A Foundation Guide

Published 1998 by
WATERSIDE PRESS
Domum Road
Winchester SO23 9NN
Telephone or Fax 01962 855567
INTERNET:106025.1020@compuserve.com

With the support of the Barrow Cadbury Trust

Copyright Susan Stewart. All rights reserved. No part of this work may be reproduced or stored in any retrieval system or transmitted by any means without the express permission in writing of the copyright holder

ISBN Paperback 1 872 870 65 1   ˙

Cataloguing-in-Publication Data A catalogue record for this book can be obtained from the British Library

Printing and binding Antony Rowe Ltd, Chippenham

Cover design John Good Holbrook Ltd, Coventry

Conflict Resolution
A Foundation Guide

Susan Stewart

WATERSIDE PRESS
WINCHESTER

The following abbreviations are used in this work

ACAS   Advisory, Conciliation and Arbitration Service

ADR   Alternative dispute resolution

AVP   Alternatives to Violence Project

CAB   Citizens' Advice Bureau

CEDR   Centre for Dispute Resolution

CIA   Chartered Institute of Arbitrators

EAP   Education Advisory Programme of Quaker Peace and Service

EMP   Elder Mediation Project

EMU   Education for Mutual Understanding

ENCORE   European Network for Conflict Resolution in Education

FGC   Family Group Conference (or Conferencing)

FIRM   Forum for Initiatives in Reparation and Mediation

FLA   Family Law Act

FMA   Family Mediators' Association

HATOS   Housing Associations' Tenants' Ombudsman Service

INCORE   Initiative on Conflict Resolution and Ethnicity

NACRO   National Association for the Care and Resettlement of Offenders

NCBI   National Coalition Building Institute

NCVO   National Council for Voluntary Organizations

NFM   National Family Mediation

NVQ   National Vocational Qualification

OCN   Open College Network

QPEP   Quaker Peace Education Project

QPS   Quaker Peace and Service

SACRO   Scottish Association for the Care and Resettlement of Offenders

SFLA   Solicitors' Family Law Association

UNESCO   United Nations Educational, Scientific and Cultural Organization

UNU   United Nations University

VORP   Victim-Offender Reparation Programme

Conflict Resolution A Foundation Guide

CONTENTS

Acknowledgments

In writing *Conflict Resolution: A Foundation Guide* I am indebted to various people at the University of Nottingham for their support (especially the staff in reprographics, education and the mail room) and to the Shakespeare Street Adult Education Centre which collected and transmitted the flood of returned questionnaires.

The nature and purpose of the questionnaire is described in *Chapter 3*. I am grateful to all the organizations and individuals who responded to it and was heartened both by the level of response, by its quality and by the generosity of the many people who sent additional information. A full list respondents appears in *Appendix III*.

This research—which provides the detailed evidence and source material on which the book is based—was generously funded by the Barrow Cadbury Trust, which also contributed to the costs of publication. Many thanks to the Trust and especially to Eric Adams for the confidence they placed in my idea and its execution.

Special thanks are also due to Professor Konrad Elsdon and Dr. John Reynolds, my mentors and colleagues in the Voluntary Organizations' Project, who gave me constant support and rigorously criticised the text as it emerged.

I am indebted to all who have given time, encouragement, information, contributions and criticism, and particularly to Jackie Bates, Colin Baxter, John Bishop, Val Carpenter, Priscilla Congreve, Carole Cowell, Thomas Daffern, Jill Day, Hywel Duck, Seamus Farrell, Thelma Fisher, Patricia Haward, Laura Knill, Graham Leach, Ken Lowles, Geraldine Maloney, Tony Marshall, Ruth Musgrave, Roger Sidaway, Christine Schoeck and Jerry Tyrrell. I am also grateful to those people and organizations mentioned at the end of *Chapters 4* to *14* who provided me with extra information or data relating to the topics covered by those chapters.

Last but not least, a big thank you to Arabella Stewart, Charles Stewart Roper and Kate Stewart Roper who kept up a steady stream of loving encouragement and provided information and insight from their various specialisms, and to Charles Clunies-Ross who not only gave invaluable guidance on the drafting of the questionnaire and the processing of the returns but provided the initial push which propelled me from talking about the project into doing the research and writing the book.

Any shortcomings are my own—but if the book provides a starting point for practitioners, students and other people wishing to learn about or develop an interest in conflict resolution it will have done its job.

Susan Stewart March 1998

CHAPTER 1

What is Conflict?

Conflicts involve struggles between two or more people over values, or competition for status, power and scarce resources.

Coser, *The Function of Social Conflict*

The pertinent issue is the need to distinguish between conflict and violence.

Darby, *What's Wrong with Conflict?*

Conflict is essential to, ineradicable from, and inevitable in human life; and the source, cause and process of conflict can be turned from life-destroying to life-building ends.

Augsburger, *Conflict Mediation Across Cultures*

Without conflict, there would be no call for conflict resolution. Before embarking on a review of strategies for resolving conflict, it is helpful to examine the phenomenon of conflict itself. Many analyses of conflict have been suggested and the study of conflict as an academic discipline flourishes. Conflict is not only perceived as destructive and harmful and requiring resolution, but also as constructive, challenging and dynamic, acting as a catalyst for change.

This chapter contains a short summary of theories of conflict and outlines some of the main ideas about its origins and nature.

CONFLICT IN SOCIAL THEORY

Conflict or consensus are the contrasting themes of two broad streams of social theory; *conflict* dominates the Marxist view of society and *consensus* characterises the liberal, functionalist perspective.

The Marxist perspective

Karl Marx, for good or ill, influenced all subsequent sociological, political, economic, ideological and historical thinking; all theories post Marx have had to take Marxism into account. He argued that 'relations of production' form the basis of society. Those who own the means of production—the capitalists—make profit by exploiting the surplus labour of those who produce goods—the workers. The relations of production are thus the cause and arena of inevitable class conflict which is the driving force of history. Relations of production form the foundation for the legal, political and ideological superstructure of the state, all of which reflect and express class interests and so the law, politics and ideas are equally arenas of conflict.

[Marxist theory has been reworked and refined, notably by Antonio Gramsci,] to include domination and subordination, as well as exploitation, of one class by another as causes of social conflict.

> Gramsci used the term 'hegemony' to refer to the moment when a ruling class is able not only to *coerce* a subordinate class to conform to its interests but to exert a 'hegemony' or 'total social authority' over subordinate classes ... A hegemonic cultural order tries to *frame* all competing definitions of the world within *its* range. It provides the horizon of thought and action within which conflicts are fought through, appropriated (i.e. experienced), obscured (i.e. concealed as a 'national interest' which should unite all conflicting parties) or contained (i.e. settled to the profit of the ruling class). A hegemonic order prescribes, not the specific content of ideas, but the *limits* within which ideas and conflicts move and are resolved.[1]

Gramsci argued in his *Prison Notebooks* (written when incarcerated by the Fascist regime in Italy between 1927 and his death in 1937) that since the Industrial Revolution, the bourgeois capitalist class had assumed hegemony as the ruling class, dominating and subordinating the working classes, and by education and propaganda successfully won the active consent of those it ruled. This confuses the clarity of the pure Marxian class struggle and replaces simple confrontation between antagonistic classes by a chaos of conflicts between different groups and interests, based on status as well as economic advantage, competing for power and space. The dominance of the bourgeois hegemony persists until the formation of an alliance of interests strong enough to overthrow it.

Sociologists who follow a theoretical standpoint based on Marxism see society in perpetual division and tension which from time to time breaks out into violence. The outcome of conflict can be good if it results in victory for the oppressed and the defeat of the oppressors, or, as Augsburger believes, it 'can be turned from life-destoying to life-building ends'.[2]

The liberal, functionalist perspective

The other main sociological theory—the liberal, functionalist perspective—focuses on the function of a social practice or institution, emphasising the contribution each part makes to the continuation of the

---

[1] Bennett, T. *et al*, *Culture, Ideology and Social Process*, p. 59

[2] Augsburger, D. A., *Conflict Mediation Across Cultures: Pathways and Patterns*

whole. Society is compared to the body which is made up of interdependent parts which depend on each other for the healthy working of the whole. The functionalist, following the work of Emile Durkheim and more recently Talcott Parsons, emphasises the inherent order, harmony and wholeness of society. In this consensus interpretation, collaboration based on mutual advantage and shared values is the healthy norm and conflict is pathological and damaging and must be resolved and repaired in order to restore harmony and well-being.

The consensus view is the preferred model of conflict in modern sociological theory though some sociologists are critical both of Marxist theories and functionalist perspective, seeing social relations as inherently antagonistic. The evidence of history suggests that conflict is more characteristic of human behaviour than is harmony.

THE VOCABULARY OF CONFLICT

There are many synonyms for conflict which describe its varied manifestations: *war, battle, strife, feud, collision, a fight, a struggle, a skirmish, a contest, an engagement* and *combat* all imply some form of physical violence. *Discord, protest, debate, dispute, disagreement, dissension, argument, confrontation, a quarrel or a difference of opinion* suggest conflict using spoken or written words with different intensities of feeling, which may escalate into physical violence or may be settled amicably. These are only a selection of the words which describe conflict. Such is the power of words that just reading them can evoke feelings of danger and action. Words with violent connotations are used to describe situations for example in politics and in competitive sport. Metaphors such as 'the cut-and-thrust of political debate' and 'the match carried the resonance of past battles' use militaristic language which is dynamic, powerful and expressive of the male qualities in human nature.

The vocabulary of peace, collaboration and co-operation is by contrast calm, static and expressive of female qualities. Words such as *friendship, amity, concord, harmony, quiet, stillness, tranquillity* and *serenity* evoke quite different feelings from the words of conflict. They describe states of repose and thoughtful meditation which can be more powerful and constructive than the noise and mindless action of conflict.

But first people have to stop and listen.

CAUSES OF CONFLICT

As suggested by the quotation from Coser at the start of this chapter, conflict arises from an imbalance in interests, power and resources between people which can be explained by application of the preferred social theory. Human beings have needs, which Maslow usefully categorised in order of priority, starting with the universal need for food and warmth, through safety and a sense of love and belonging to the 'higher' needs of self-esteem, self actualisation and understanding and knowledge.[3] When people perceive that they have needs which are not being met, and which they can see that other people enjoy, then the 'have-nots' may engage in a struggle with the 'haves' to achieve their goals. Unequal distribution of resources creates *structural* causes of conflict. For example:

- hungry people will compete for food
- people denied civil rights will fight for freedom
- people crowded into a small poor land will fight to gain space; and
- people will fight to defend their property and high standard of living.

In the world today, the potential for conflict is increasing as the rich get richer and the poor poorer.

People also engage in conflict about *ideologies* or ideas and beliefs. *Ideological* conflicts occur on a large scale between religious faiths or political systems, or may break out on a small scale between neighbours of different cultural traditions.

Emotions—dimensions and responses

Everyone varies in their circumstances: their resources, prospects, ideas and beliefs. Greater ease of communication makes people aware of differences between living styles and this recognition has both intellectual and emotional components; people would not fight if they did not *feel* injustice and did not have feelings about their situation. Without the spark of *emotion*, the fire of conflict would not blaze. An emotion and its physical expression are closely linked and are simultaneously triggered in reaction to people and situations as they are perceived and experienced. There are some 400 names for human emotions. Many describe basic reaction patterns: *joy, acceptance, fear,*

---

[3] Maslow, A. H., 'A Theory of Human Motivation'

surprise, sadness, disgust, anger and anticipation.[4] Each of these is the source of a dimension of emotions—the fear dimension, sadness dimension and so on—and an ingredient in complex mixed emotional states. Emotions produce behaviour patterns which signal motivations and intentions from one person to another and these produce reactions. Behaviour which is perceived as threatening may evoke defensive, angry and hurt feelings which in turn may provoke guilt, aggression and hostility. Extreme emotional responses escalate a conflict into physical violence which is beyond the control of the combatants.

A mixture of causes

Conflicts between individuals and groups of people usually have a mixture of causes which can be analysed as:

- structural
- ideological
- behavioural; and
- emotional.

Some of these may be based on misinformation, misunderstanding and misperceptions, others may be based on prejudice. Some may be superficial and amenable to change; others so deep-seated that no improvement is foreseeable. Sometimes the obvious causes are only an excuse for a conflict and the real causes lie much deeper, unspoken, unacknowledged and even unrecognised. However apparently irrational, mistaken and misdirected, the feelings of the disputants are crucial to any analysis of the underlying issues.

LATENT CONFLICT

Conflict sometimes remains repressed and unspoken when it could be argued that it would be better brought into the open. Such latent conflict arises when it is felt preferable to bear the pain of disharmony silently than to suffer the consequences of open conflict. People may accept a measure of injustice and unfairness either from indifference or because to take action to challenge the situation might jeopardise other advantageous aspects of their lives. It is often the weak and vulnerable who find themselves in such situations—such as women who endure intolerable family situations for the sake of their young children; or people who put up with harassment in the workplace in order to keep their jobs.

---

[4] Hochschild A. R., *The Managed Heart*, Appendices A and B

11

HANDLING CONFLICT

Conflict is a present reality and no consensus theory about how society should work will wish conflict away. At a global level, the causes of conflict are too many and too deeply entrenched for quick resolution, though there are groups and movements who work indefatigably to achieve world peace. On local and personal levels, greater understanding of the reasons for conflict, willingness to engage in dialogue, to listen to the points of view of other people and to search for collaborative ways of working have created opportunities in many fields for handling conflict in such a way that it does not escalate into violence.

Conflict resolution strategies

By using conflict resolution strategies, often with the help of skilled facilitators, people can be supported and encouraged actively to seek permanent solutions to their disputes. This book describes a variety of such strategies as well as examining in closer detail the ideas, methods, projects, education and research which are currently contributing to the work of conflict resolution.

SOURCES AND FURTHER READING: *Chapter 1*

Augsburger, D. A., *Conflict Mediation Across Cultures: Pathways and Patterns*, 1992
Bennett, T, Martin, G, Mercer, C and Woollacott, J. (Eds.), *Culture, Ideology and Social Process*, 1981
Coser, L., *The Functions of Social Conflict*, 1956
Crawley, J., *Constructive Conflict Management: Managing to Make a Difference*, 1992
Darby, J., *What's Wrong with Conflict*, 1994
Giddens, A., *Durkheim*, 1978
Giddens, A., *Sociology*, 1989
Hamilton, P., *Talcott Parsons*, 1983
Hochschild, A. R., *The Managed Heart*, 1983
Joll, J., *Gramsci*, 1977
Maslow, A. H., 'A Theory of Human Motivation', *Psychology Review* 50, 370-396, 1943
Parkin, F., *Durkheim*, 1992.

CHAPTER 2

trategies for Resolving Conflict

e real issue is not the existence of conflict but how it is handled.

Darby, *What's Wrong with Conflict?*

um legem vincit et amor iudicium Agreement prevails over law and love
judgment.

Laws of Henry I, 1100-1135

Jaw-jaw is better than war-war.

Winston Churchill

All the activity described in this book assumes that conflict should be
dealt with in a non-violent, non-confrontational and non-adversarial
way and should leave the disputants always in control. Clearly conflict
can cause violence, either in words or in deeds. At the extreme end of
the spectrum, conflict between two ethnic groups can be ended when
one group eliminates the other, and history has examples: the
indigenous people of the Caribbean islands were wiped out by the
conquistadores, either by massacre or the diseases they brought with
them; some native American tribes were annihilated by the incoming
white invaders and others were reduced to a pitiful remnant. Modern
examples of genocide in Bosnia, Ruanda and Burundi have been
graphically and horrifyingly reported by the news media.

Violent actions lead to violent responses and a renewing cycle of
conflict, such as raids and counter raids in the Debatable Lands between
Scotland and England in the sixteenth and seventeenth centuries or
blood feuds in Anglo-Saxon England or modern Italy. Wars of words
can lead to protracted lawsuits and damage done in the courts can
wreck lives as effectively as duels fought with swords and pistols.

A RANGE OF STRATEGIES

In this chapter the various strategies aimed at resolving conflict are
identified and described, together with an analysis of the processes
which have come to be attached to each. Formalised analysis of conflict
resolution strategies was pioneered in the United States and much
literature of the literature and research is American. Learning from
American models, conflict resolution philosophy and strategy

developed in Britain from the 1970s, reworked to relate more closely to the British context; and in other countries, such as Germany, Holland and Switzerland. International networks such as ENCORE (European Network for Conflict Resolution in Education) provide forums through which innovative work can be shared. This book focuses on the position in the United Kingdom, but with some reference to wider horizons—not least as a reminder that conflict resolution is a world-wide activity.

However, before examining these strategies (and the vocabulary of modern alternative dispute resolution), an outline of the development of law as a means of resolving disputes without recourse to violence is instructive. Attention is also drawn to examples of the use of other historic alternative strategies.

LAW AND THE RESOLUTION OF DISPUTES

The benefits of non-violent settlement of conflict can be easily accepted by the weak; the powerful may need more pressure to persuade them that a peaceful settlement is in their interests too. The articulation of law was the first step in making the powerful and quarrelsome accept non-violent ways of settling disputes. The laws of King Ine (c. 690) fixed the financial compensation rate or *wergild* for murder according to the status of the victim: 1,200 shillings to the relative of a well born warrior; a mere 200 shillings for a lowly tiller of the soil. 'If someone hits a man on the nose, it will cost him a shilling' is an example of the scale of compensation for injury. The laws of Alfred (871-99) set *wergilds* for all bodily injuries down to the loss of a toenail. The threat of revenge remained as a disincentive to violence, whilst compensation reinforced the vested interest of both kindred in peace.

Perpetrators of crime had to be caught, so every Anglo-Saxon adult male was obliged by law to belong to a *tithing* of ten men who had collective responsibility for each other's behaviour and fines. As kings became more powerful, they were able to enforce the king's peace; violence against a king's subject was violence against the king himself and penalties were levied for breaches of the peace.

Feudal law favoured judicial duels as a means of settling disputes and the use of ordeals to sort out the guilty from the innocent. In the early thirteenth century the church decreed that ordeals were theologically unsound so in England the tradition of collective responsibility and decision-making in the form of a jury of peers became an integral part of the criminal justice process. For civil cases a variety of formulae were developed which could be used in the courts to decide the rights and wrongs of possession of land in an *adversarial* but non-violent way. Men who were experts in the detail of the law started to act as attorneys for protagonists in cases and established themselves as professional lawyers with a vested interest in adversarial litigation. Dispute settlement became formalised and 'law and procedure bound'; ways of resolving conflict polarised between violence outside the law and rigid, *confrontational* procedures within it.

Alternatives to 'going to law'

Alongside the development of law as the means of resolving disputes without recourse to violence, alternative means of settling conflict were sometimes used. The medieval perspective is well expressed by the quotation from the Laws of Henry I already set out at the beginning of this chapter: 'Agreement prevails over law and love over judgment.' Medieval disputants had a choice and were well aware of it. They could take a dispute to law and judgment or they could use alternative solutions 'to proceed by love, if the parties wish to have perfect freedom of friends to come and go.'

Lovedays and heralds

Lovedays and heralds are examples of alternative dispute resolution studied in different cultures and periods by anthropologists and historians.

Instead of pursuing a case by way of a lawsuit, disputants could decide to ask for a loveday, 'a day of reconciliation'. Sometimes a court would declare a general loveday to give disputants in all the cases before it a chance to settle their differences 'out of court'. Compromises might be reached through direct negotiation, through mediation by third parties or by arbitration before a respected senior member of the community. In working out a settlement regarded as equitable by both sides, strict legal rights might give way to custom and the shared cultural values of the community. Records of lovedays are rare because they were outside the formal business of the court, and legal innovations of the later medieval period, including the development of equity (a system running parallel to civil law and based on principles of fairness), seem to have curtailed community participation in settlements in favour of legal procedures conducted by professional lawyers operating within the judicial system.

The use of third parties as mediators was well developed in the institution of heralds. In Shakespeare's *Henry V*, Mountjoy gives a dramatic representation of the herald first giving voice to the French dauphin's point of view, and after the battle negotiating for permission to search for casualties.

DEVELOPMENT OF ALTERNATIVE STRATEGIES

In describing the strategies of the medieval loveday, the vocabulary of alternative dispute resolution (ADR) has crept in virtually unawares. The development and use of *alternative* dispute resolution strategies in modern times is advocated both as *alternative to violence* and as an *alternative to adversarial litigation*. When ADR techniques are under discussion, they should always be examined by asking: 'Alternative to what?'

Adjudication
As outlined above, historically the law developed as the first alternative to violent resolution of disputes. A conflict brought before the law, whether in a criminal court (where the dispute is between the perpetrator of a crime and the state) or in a civil court (where the dispute is between two private parties) is subject to *adjudication*. The evidence is laid out by each side, usually through the auspices of legal experts, before a judge, jury, bench of magistrates, or a tribunal (a quasi-judicial hearing). On the basis of the evidence, a decision is reached following law and legal precedent which is binding on the parties (though open to appeal, in some instances right up to the Court of Appeal and House of Lords). The court's decision can be enforced by the use of various coercive powers and in criminal cases offenders face penal sanctions. The process is adversarial. Usually, lawyers representing the parties argue the case in the best interests of their client, each seeking 'a win'—and consequent defeat for their opponent.

If the lawyer for one party perceives that things are going badly for his or her own client, he or she may, in a civil case, go for an out-of-court settlement rather than pursue judgment in court. This might involve weighing the likely prospects of an award of damages against the risk of a crippling award of costs if the case goes against the client. In a criminal case, it may involve a change of plea from 'not guilty' to 'guilty'; or a plea of guilty to a lesser offence (sometimes called a 'plea bargain'). Coupled with this, in all criminal cases the lawyer will usually seek to put forward reasons why his or her client should receive the lightest possible sentence (known as 'mitigation'). Adjudication is an alternative to violence, but not an alternative to adversarial litigation. It is most unlikely to leave all parties feeling satisfied with the outcome. In so far as the parties are dissatisfied, the conflict remains unresolved.

Arbitration
Arbitration is a method of dispute resolution in civil matters which can be agreed to by both parties, which may be binding and which can have

the force of law. Thus, a party might be obliged to go to arbitration on a particular issue as part of an agreement concerning dispute resolution procedures which he or she has previously accepted. The status of the outcome of arbitration has to be agreed by the disputants before they engage in the process. Arbitration involves the disputants laying their case before an independent, impartial but expert arbitrator who from knowledge of the law and an examination of the facts of the case makes a decision which, if the parties have so agreed, will be binding. The process removes the adversarial 'battle' witnessed in the courtroom, but is conducted within a legal context (eg a contract may require the parties to settle certain matters by arbitration). In pay and conditions disputes, the outcome of arbitration tends to fall somewhere between the last two positions adopted by the sides. *Pendulum arbitration* is a variation which requires the arbitrator to choose one of the two last positions taken by the disputants.

The Arbitration Act 1996 states that

> the object of arbitration is to obtain the fair resolution of disputes by an impartial tribunal without unnecessary delay or expense; and the parties should be free to agree how their disputes are resolved subject only to such safeguards as are necessary in the public interest.

The 1996 Act reduces the interventionist jurisdiction of the High Court over arbitrators; it recognises arbitration as a consensual process and is based on the principle that the court's role is to support arbitrators and not to try to control them. The advantages of arbitration are its fairness, speed and finality; the disadvantages are that there is no dialogue between the parties during the process and, once someone's case is made, all decision-making power lies with the arbitrator.

Mediation

Mediation is a word used to describe a great deal of ADR. Essentially, mediation is a process in which a third party, a neutral outsider to the dispute, draws the disputants to an agreed settlement of their conflict. In doing so, *mediators* act as *facilitators* to reduce difficulties which obstruct agreement and to make the process of reaching a concord easier.

A mediator is by definition 'the person in the middle' and should have no partiality to either side. Mediation cannot by its nature be compulsory and can only take place if both parties are voluntary participants. A mediator's role is to establish lines of communication and dialogue between the two parties which will lead to greater mutual understanding and in the end to an agreement which will restore or create by non-violent means, if not friendship and love, at least a future

17

relationship without conflict. Mediators can work very discreetly, by shuttle diplomacy, taking messages between disputants in the hope that common ground and common interests may be discovered. They can defuse potential distress or anger by preventing misunderstandings and correcting misconstructions put on the behaviour of one party by the other. They prevent escalation of disputes by creating a climate where talking about grievances and reasons for hostility gives vent to violent emotions and brings deep feelings out into the open without the release of physical violence. Mediators run the risk of themselves becoming targets of frustration and anger if they are perceived by one side to be favouring the other.

After laying the foundations with patient listening and sharing of information and feelings, mediators hope to bring the disputants together 'to sit down round a table' to address their problems face-to-face. These frequently used words—to sit down round a table—in themselves send a powerful message. Disputants cannot engage in physical violence if they are sitting down; round a table they are all equal and symbols of power are left outside the room. Parties remain free to quit the process and walk out of face-to-face meetings at any time. Part of the mediator's skill is to keep the disputants communicating—either by *indirect* mediation between the parties or by bringing about *direct* mediation between disputants. Brought together in the same room, mediators will aim in the end to produce an agreement, preferably written down, which both parties will sign and intend to keep. Mediators may then, if the parties wish, monitor the agreement to make sure that it is observed.

To be accepted by both parties, a mediator has to be:

- totally impartial, showing no preference or favours to either side
- fair and non-judgmental, treating each side equally; and
- empathetic, showing respect to each side by total understanding of their point of view and total confidentiality with regard to information and feelings revealed.

By creating 'a level playing field' on which the parties have equal opportunity to state their case, express their feelings and declare their aspirations and needs, the mediator can redress any power imbalance that may exist between the disputants.

The mediator's role is to be a sounding board and a mouthpiece, to give no advice and to create an atmosphere in which the parties are empowered to solve their own problems and find their own solutions. Mediators may suggest options (the same to each party) but should not advise or influence the parties in their choices. Mediators may intervene more creatively to give information, to point out directions which the parties could explore and to provide facts about, for example, rights and benefits. As a go-between, the mediator can interpret messages in constructive ways and, while giving the same information and knowledge to both parties, edge them closer to agreement.

The classic mediation process involves:

- initial interviews with each party separately
- the arrangement of a face-to-face meeting at which each party tells his or her story and articulates feelings and aspirations
- the discovery of options
- the finding of common ground and common interests; and
- the framing of an agreement.

In practice, face-to-face meetings happen in only a minority of mediations and most disputants prefer to use the mediator's skills as a go-between to bring about an agreement. The desired outcome of the mediation process is a resolution of the conflict with healing of the emotional hurt that the conflict has caused. At the least, the process should lay the foundation for improvement in relations between the parties in the future.

TERMINOLOGY

The following terminology may be encountered in relation to mediation and other forms of ADR:

- *Family mediation*
  This the same process working to resolve conflicts within a family, many of which occur at the time that partners are separating or divorcing. Family mediators are especially concerned about the future wellbeing of any children caught up in the conflict and they may act as advocates of the children's point ot view, pointing out their needs and rights. *Family Mediation* is the subject matter of *Chapter 4.*

- *Consensus-building*
  A term used for mediation which involves a number of interested parties or stake-holders in a dispute. A mediator working to build a consensus between different interest groups may start the process with telephone interviews and follow up with a conference of representatives from all the parties involved. Consensus-building is a technique of mediation suited to

resolving conflicts which involve a number of strongly held points of view; this form of mediation is sometimes referred to as *facilitation*. In commercial mediation, the final face-to-face meeting has some features of a conference where the mediator facilitates the process and conducts some intense shuttle diplomacy in separate *caucus* meetings. A commercial mediator is in the position of a go-between in a negotiation process.

- *Reparation*
  Reparation is linked with mediation in the field of victim-offender mediation. To make reparation is to make amends for wrong doing. Part of mediation and reparation between the victim of a crime and the perpetrator involves the payment of appropriate reparation by the perpetrator to the victim. This may be in the form of an apology, and payment or a service. Mediation and reparation demand the agreement of both parties, but direct mediation is quite unusual as the feelings involved are usually very intense. A lot of work is directed towards healing the hurt of the victim and changing the attitudes and behaviour of the perpetrator.

- *Counselling and therapy*
  These are terms for intensive work by professional specialists with individuals and small groups of people who have personal problems. In counselling and therapy, the client is engaged in a search for understanding of his or her own personal problems and emotions and is seeking to come to terms with and accept and value the self. Although some of the skills such as empathetic listening and some qualities such as confidentiality and non-judgmental acceptance are common to counselling and mediation, the purpose and outcomes of these processes are very different and should not be confused.

- *Conciliation and reconciliation*
  Conciliation and reconciliation are strategies involving third party intervention and are very similar to mediation. Indeed the terms often seem to be used interchangeably. A conciliator will clarify issues and liaise between parties but be less active than a mediator in suggesting options for the solution of a dispute. Conciliation implies a coming together of parties where interests are anyway moving closer and where there is already a measure of goodwill. Reconciliation implies the bringing together of disputants who were once friends or partners and have fallen out.

These terms, like mediation, are used in a variety of contexts with slightly different shades of meaning and should be approached with care. In North America, conciliation is used to describe indirect mediation, or seeing the parties separately; this should be borne in mind when reading North American publications.

- *Peacemaking and peacekeeping*
  These terms are generally used for the peace processes conducted through independent third parties which aim to resolve armed conflicts which may be, for example, wars between groups within a state, or between a regional group striving for independence and a central government or between different nation states. The terms may also be used in connection with hostage situations. Both these terms describe alternatives to violence.
  Peacemaking is the part of the process which is often conducted with little publicity. To have a chance of success, peacemakers acting as diplomats, negotiators and mediators between the two (or more) sides will have to be trusted by all participants and be able to move freely between them, opening up channels of communication and seeking areas of common understanding and agreement. The outcome of peacemaking usually only becomes public knowledge after months, maybe years, of patient work. Recent examples would be the Dayton agreement between the warring groups in Bosnia and the Oslo Accord between Israel and the Palestine authorities. Both these were public statements of the results of a process lasting years with peacemakers working step by step to build a basis of mutual trust and seizing significant moments in the armed struggle when the combatants seemed most ready to move forward from armed conflict to a period of truce and further negotiation.
  Peacekeeping moves the process on to a stage when the search for a negotiated peaceful co-existence is supported by the beginnings of social and economic reconstruction. This phase will often require the supervision of monitors and may need enforcement by a neutral force to allow the restoration of civilian judicial and political processes. A culture of violence has to be transformed into a stable, non-violent normality in which the hearts and minds of the former combatants are convinced of the benefits of permanent peace.

- *Negotiation*
  Negotiation is the conflict resolution strategy in which direct bargaining takes place between the parties in a dispute, without

21

the intervention of third parties. As a technique of ADR it is associated with industrial disputes in which expert negotiators from and on behalf of each side use a formalised structure of moves and counter-moves to bring the two sides close enough together for a bargain to be struck. It is sometimes referred to as 'give-and-take' or 'give-and-get', as each side gives a little and takes a little to get a balanced outcome in which both can claim to be winners.

Negotiation is essentially a form of bargaining which can take place within other forms of ADR. Settlement of conflict involves compromise and concession on each side; each party is likely to have to give up something in order to gain something more important. In mediation and consensus-building, the mediator is the facilitator of negotiation and in media reports these terms are often used interchangeably.

• *Conflict prevention*
This term describes a mixture of negotiation, good communication, creative problem-solving and consensus-building used early in a situation to prevent the development of conflict. It is part of good management practice and good staff relations. Practices and structures which are perceived as open and fair and which empower people to participate in decision-making are good conflict prevention strategies.

• *Conflict avoidance*
This term may also be used to describe strategies for preventing the development of disputes. Conflict avoidance can also describe a reluctance to address causes of dispute and even a denial that there is a problem. This may be a legitimate strategy for averting confrontation and while a conflict is postponed, circumstances may change to alter people's attitudes and expectations. An example of legitimate conflict avoidance was the decision of the international peacemaker in February 1997 not to decide to whom to award the administrative control of the town of Brcko in Bosnia so that there were no winners and no losers and a renewed outbreak of war was avoided.

Conflict avoidance and conflict tolerance can however be destructive when emotions are denied and feelings suppressed in a way which encourages them to build up under pressure ready to break out more violently in response to a trigger in the future. It can also result in loss of control over outcomes as other parties in a dispute take initiatives and make decisions unilaterally.

UNIVERSAL OR CULTURE-SPECIFIC?

Are ADR strategies universal or culture-specific? John Paul Lederach suggests that assumptions were too readily made in North American development that the conflict resolution process is culturally neutral.

> In my experience, the prescriptive nature of our methodology makes little if any adjustment as we move across cultural and class lines. Metaphorically, we tend to translate our materials into another language rather than create them in situ.[1]

He asserts that processes of expressing and handling conflict are embedded in cultural assumptions which must be identified and acknowledged for world peace-making to be successful. The models of ADR which work in one cultural tradition may not transfer easily to another. It follows that ways in which different cultures perceive conflict, express feelings and needs, use verbal and body language and value relationships should be integral to the peace-making processes if they are to bring about the conflict transformation which will make them sustainable and permanent.

OUTCOMES OF ADR

A number of terms are used to describe the outcomes of ADR. A dispute might be *settled*, a conflict may be *resolved*, both these implying that the conflict has been sorted out once and for all. *Consensus* implies agreement on main issues and ways forward rather than resolution of the causes of conflict. *Defusion* or *management of conflict* suggest that the heat has been taken out of the situation for the time being, but beneath the surface there is potential for the outbreak of further conflict. *Conflict transformation* and *healing* are used to describe the ideal outcomes of the process whereby the attitudes, feelings and behaviour of the disputants are so changed that lasting peace is assured. There is ongoing debate on how far mediation can or should aim to have a transformative purpose, bringing about therapeutic change that is deeper than the pragmatic resolution of the conflict situation.

---

[1] Lederach J. P., *Preparing for Peace: Conflict Transformation Across Cultures*, p. 33

CONCLUSION

In this chapter, the main strategies of ADR and the vocabulary associated with them have been reviewed. The aim of all ADR is to use constructive and creative strategies to achieve change in a non-violent way from a situation of conflict to an environment of peace. The advantages of ADR strategies are that they provide disputants with accessible, fair and cheap processes for resolving their conflicts which satisfy feelings of natural justice and hold out the possibility of a future relationship. They empower people to make their own decisions and find their own solutions. Essentially all ADR seeks to develop full, free and equitable communication, understanding and mutual trust and respect between disputants in order to achieve outcomes that are fair, just and permanent.

SOURCES AND FURTHER READING: *Chapter 2*

Acland, A. F., *Resolving Disputes Without Going to Court, 1995*
Bevan, A., *Alternative Dispute Resolution: A Lawyer's Guide to Mediation and Other Forms of Dispute Resolution, 1992*
Bossy, J. (Ed.), *Disputes and Settlements: Law and Human Relations in the West, 1983*
Davis W. and Fouracre, P. (Eds.), *Settlement of Disputes in Early Medieval Europe, 1986*
Lederach, J. P., *Preparing for Peace: Conflict Transformation Across Cultures, 1995*
Mackie, K. N. (Ed.), *A Handbook of Dispute Resolution: ADR in Action, 1991*
Moore, C. W., *The Mediation Process: Practical Strategies for Resolving Conflict, 1986*
Powell, E., *Kingship, Law and Society: Criminal Justice in the Reign of Henry V, 1989* (especially *Chapter 4,* 'Law, Politics and Dispute Settlement in Local Society').

CHAPTER 3

Approach to the Territory

At first it was simply ignored, then it was regarded as eccentric, dangerous even. Now it has become impossible to find anyone who had ever opposed it. Such has been the shift in attitude towards alternative dispute resolution techniques . . .

Article in the *Financial Times*, 5 November 1996

The ensuing chapters explore various aspects of conflict resolution. The information which they contain is grounded in the results of a wide-ranging survey carried out between September 1996 and March 1997, the objective of which was to chart and explore the 'territory' of alternative dispute resolution (ADR) in the United Kingdom. This chapter describes how that enquiry was conducted and outlines its main findings.

The survey starts close to home, in the family and local community, where conflict arises between individuals within a household or between people living in a neighbourhood. Discussion then extends outward to encompass the public areas of work, commercial and corporate activity, before moving, finally, on to the world stage.

Individuals, families, neighbours and communities

Conflict at the most intensely interpersonal level involves partners and other family members for whom it threatens serious disruption if not total destruction of their pattern of life. The emotionally charged content of such conflicts can be escalated by adversarial confrontation and can also cause trauma to all those caught up in them. With recognition of the damaging consequences of embattled family conflict, alternative dispute resolution services have been and are increasingly being developed—pursuant to the Family Law Act 1996—have been built into the legal process.

Moving outward from the family, neighbours are the next closest protagonists of conflict. Disputes between neighbours arise from a perception of invasion by any means of the living space of one person by another. They range from the petty to the disastrous, from the trivial to the very costly, but of whatever dimension they disturb the harmony and well-being of the community. The development of neighbourhood mediation services is the community response to neighbourhood conflict. Of immediate concern to individuals and families, conflict situations may arise, for example:

- between parents and the schools attended by their children
- within peer groups
- between older and younger people in a community
- between the perpetrators of crime and their victims.

These are all areas within which the development of ADR will be examined in the following chapters.

World of work
Conflict in the worlds of work and commerce ranges from:

- business in dispute with business
- workforce collectively in conflict with management
- employees individually making claims against employers
- customers in conflict with suppliers; to
- clients in conflict with service providers.

The variety of ADR options open to disputants is increasingly perceived, as explained by the *Financial Times* in the article quoted at the head of this chapter, as preferable to meeting the costs, in legal fees, compensation claims, and loss of time and wages, of pursuing disputes *adversarially*.

Cross-cultural mediation and peacemaking
Finally the survey turns to cross-cultural mediation and peacemaking. Efforts at making and keeping peace between ethnic and religious groups and between nations are often headline news. Crises involving the taking of hostages stretch the skills of mediators. National and international agencies and mechanisms for the prevention or cessation of hostilities do not always succeed but try to build bridges and create a framework for peaceful co-existence. Issues arising from the need for the resolution of environmental conflict may be the most significant for the future of life on this planet.

ASSEMBLING UP TO DATE INFORMATION

Information about current projects and programmes in the United Kingdom was obtained by means of a questionnaire. Via an introductory letter, potential respondents were introduced to the purpose of the research, invited to complete the questionnaire and asked to send appropriate and relevant literature along with their response. The questionnaire enquired about the type of organization (statutory, voluntary or private) and about its involvement in different fields of conflict management and ADR. It asked what services the organization provided, about the number of staff and volunteers and their roles, training in relevant skills and qualifications. Some final questions asked about research undertaken and publications produced. The questionnaire itself is set out in *Appendix I* to this work and further details of how the survey was conducted in *Appendix II*.

Fields of activity

In the survey, 186 respondents (91 per cent) declared that the work of their organization included conflict management, indicating between them activity in 35 fields distributed as shown in *Table 3.1* overleaf.

It can be seen that the six main fields set out at the head of the table were all well represented in the responses. The 29 other specialisms declared in response to the question 'Other ADR, please specify' indicate the wide applicability of ADR. Many respondents clearly felt it important to particularise their specialism or their specific client group, reflecting their response to need and often indicating innovative work and specialist skills. The growing field of work in schools and with young people is particularly well represented. The quality of information given on the questionnaire forms was generally good and helpful and 120 respondents (59 per cent) included supplementary leaflets, reports and other documentation with their responses, much of the information generously detailed. The majority of respondents declared a willingness to a follow up by way of a telephone interview, if further information was required. An initial assessment indicated that 17 respondents certainly and a further 50 or so possibly might have useful extra information to give.

Additional contacts and information

In addition to information on the questionnaires and the extra documentation sent by respondents, 38 in-depth contacts were made across the entire range of fields of activity. Twenty-one of these involved meetings with individuals or groups; four attendance at conferences; the other 13 were telephone interviews and/or an exchange of letters and the supply of reports. These contacts had the purpose of gathering more detailed information about each field and finding examples and case studies with which to illustrate the research. Six of the contacts—including one of the conferences—covered the field of environmental mediation (which was not represented in the questionnaire responses). A full list of respondents and supplementary contacts is given in *Appendix III*.

27

	Number
Six main options given in the questionnaire	
Neighbourhood mediation	70
Family mediation	53
Victim-offender mediation	30
Industrial-commercial mediation	21
Negotiation-conciliation services	38
Complaints-grievance procedures	47
	259
Other categories specified by the respondents themselves	
Schools	17
Youth	8
Peer mediation	3
Elderly	1
Post-adoption	1
Tenant/landlord disputes	3
Domestic violence	3
Workplace	2
Group	2
Disabilities	3
Mental health	1
Debt	1
Religious	4
Inter-religious	3
Multi-cultural-cross-cultural	4
Stress management	1
Advocacy	3
Consultancy	4
Training	9
Counselling	11
Research	7
International	3
'Named person' in special needs cases	2
Arbitration service	1
Consensus facilitation	1
Victim-accused	1
Offender-community	1
Between statutory agencies	1
With voluntary organizations	4
	103
Total	362

Table 3.1: Fields of Activity

THE INFORMATION IN CONTEXT

In the chapters that follow, the information collected in questionnaires, literature, interviews and from observation is discussed and evaluated field by field under the following main heads:

- Family Mediation: *Chapter 4*
- Mediation Between Neighbours: *Chapter 5*
- Restorative Justice: *Chapter 6*
- Mediation in Schools: *Chapter 7*
- Cross-Cultural and Multi-Faith Mediation: *Chapter 8*
- Environmental Conflict: *Chapter 9*
- David and Goliath: *Chapter 10*
- The World of Work: *Chapter 11*

In several of these chapters, detailed case studies or profiles exemplify and illuminate a general outline of the topic.

Training and research
A significant portion of the questionnaire was devoted to an enquiry into training and research. The responses disclosed that 121 of the organizations (59 per cent) provide training or courses in mediation/ADR and 61 (30 per cent) initiate or participate in research. Training and research are discussed in *Chapters 12* and *13*.

Issues arising
Comments and observations arising from the responses are made in *Chapter 14, Issues for the Future.*

CHAPTER 4

Family Mediation

The system of resolving disputes through partisan arms length negotiations draws families into conflict at a time of considerable stress in their lives. Family mediation offers an alternative which has the effect of reducing tension while encouraging a couple to reach agreement on the way they must inevitably reorganize their lives and those of their children. Out of court mediation has been shown to have some particularly positive effects.

Looking to the Future: Mediation and the Ground for Divorce (1993)

With it (the passage of the Family Law Act 1996) the future place of family mediation within the divorce law of this country is secured.

Thelma Fisher, *National Family Mediation Annual Report* (1996)

In the two and a half years between the publication by the Lord Chancellor's Department of the consultation paper *Looking to the Future: Mediation and the Ground for Divorce* and the long awaited Family Law Act 1996 in July of that year, debate focused on the use of alternative dispute resolution strategies to manage and ameliorate the conflicts of marriage breakdown. A third of the consultation paper was devoted to family mediation, how it might work and what it would cost. Overlapping with that debate and rising to a crescendo as the 1997 election approached, affirmation of support for the family and 'family values' became the vociferous creed of politicians from all parties. It might be expected that mediation and other dispute resolution strategies to help families in crisis would flourish and expand both in the cause of reforming the procedures of divorce and as a way of supporting and strengthening the family as the core unit in society.

In this chapter the diversity of family mediation and ADR strategies is outlined, focusing first on divorce mediation—a specific and high profile sub-section of family mediation. Strategies and interventions for strengthening family units are then reviewed.

Questionnaire responses
A wide range of expertise is called upon to attempt management and resolution of disharmony within the family. Fifty-three respondents to the questionnaire (see *Chapter 3*) indicated family mediation as their main activity or as part of it. Twenty-nine of these were from the voluntary sector, 14 were statutory agencies and ten private. Twenty-one out of the 53 responses were from organizations specialising only in

family work. One of these, National Family Mediation, represents 70 affiliated services, a sample of which responded individually to questionnaires.

Organization	Type	No of responses
Family mediation services (specialist)	Voluntary	11
Family mediation services	Private	10
Community mediation services (generalist)	Voluntary	9
Relate	Voluntary	7
Housing associations	Voluntary	2
Probation services	Statutory	6
Social services	Statutory	4
Police	Statutory	3
University (research)	Statutory	1

Table 4.1: Responses from Organizations and Agencies Active in Family Work

Relate (formerly Marriage Guidance) branches clarified the different functions of their services. Relate offers 'counselling, sexual therapy and other services to help with difficulties in marriage or in any adult couple relationship.' Although Relate counselling may lead to a resolution of a conflict, that is not its prime purpose and though some of the process skills are shared, the boundary between counselling and sexual therapy on the one hand and mediation and ADR strategies on the other should remain clear.

The Family Law Act 1996 and divorce mediation
Family mediation in divorce settlements is now enshrined in the Family Law Act 1996 which creates a framework for a more civilised divorce procedure, with mediation in a central place when it is deemed by clients and mediators as suitable. Part III of the Act sets out the structure for public funding of mediation for eligible and suitable clients and requires adherence to a code of practice on the part of mediators as a condition of Legal Aid Board contracts. The relevant provisions come into force in 1999, under which preliminary compulsory information meetings will explain to divorcing couples the advantages of mediation and the way in which the process might work. With this explanation as an integral part of the initiation of divorce proceedings, it is hoped that mediation rather than confrontational court action will become an accepted way of solving the conflicts which follow from the break up of

a marriage. In the interim, schemes for the implementation of the new procedures and funding criteria are being piloted.

The reforms in the 1996 Act are the latest response to concern expressed at prevailing levels of divorce. One in three of new marriages and 40 per cent of second marriages in Britain end in divorce. Over 150,000 couples divorce each year in England and Wales and the United Kingdom has the highest divorce rate within the European Community. As the consultation paper *Looking Into The Future* points out, there is confusion in debate between divorce and marriage breakdown. Before the easing of the divorce law in 1969, marriage breakdowns resulted in separations, either legal or *de facto*, or were concealed in unhappy households with partners and their children deadlocked in conflict. In the 1990s 'the reason why we have so many divorces is that so many marriages break down' and can be ended by legal process.

Causes and effects of marriage breakdown
The causes of marriage breakdown are debated by politicians, religious leaders, social scientists, agony aunts, chatshow hosts, journalists and 'the person in the street', and many questions are asked and answers suggested. The consequences of marriage breakdown and divorce are less controversial, and recognised as the next most stressful life experience after bereavement. The effect on children is particularly severe; during 1992 in England and Wales around 150,000 children aged under 16 were affected by divorce, 57,000 of them aged under five—and research shows that the life chances of children from broken homes are severely damaged. In terms of financial cost, legal aid for divorce cases alone costs around £180 million a year (1997) and the total overall cost of marriage breakdown to the public purse has been estimated at well over £1 billion a year. A driving force behind the emphasis on mediation in the Family Law Act might cynically be interpreted as financial economy. The Green Paper above quoted the estimated comparative costs; a legal aid funded divorce in 1992/3 cost an average of £1,565 while a mediated divorce cost on average £540.[1]

NATIONAL FAMILY MEDIATION: VOLUNTARY PERSPECTIVE

A number of separate strands of development in the 1970s foreshadowed alternative ways of resolving disputes in response to the increased divorce rate and its consequences. The government-appointed

---

[1] *Looking Into The Future: Mediation and the Ground for Divorce,* Green Paper, Lord Chancellor's Department, 1993, Cmnd. 2799, p. 72

Finer Committee in 1973 examined the situation of one-parent families and proposed a Family Court with a conciliation service to deal with contentious issues arising from divorce. Family mediation was identified in the Finer Report as the social practice and intervention required to address the new social problems, especially the needs of children, arising from the rise in the divorce rate. Family mediation was not intended by the report to be a voluntary sector service and in the early days of its development as a voluntary initiative it was expected that it would rapidly become part of the legal procedure of divorce settlements. When this did not happen, the voluntary sector was left to carry forward the concept, practice and ethical standards of family mediation as the only way to ensure that it was available to meet the needs of a growing number of people.

The first independent Family Conciliation Service was set up in Bristol in 1978. By 1981, the National Family Conciliation Council was inaugurated with 20 local services. Renamed National Family Mediation (NFM) in 1992, by the end of 1996 there were 68 affiliated local services in England and Wales (plus 12 in Scotland and Northern Ireland) with 700 mediators, providing family mediation throughout the country, dealing with about 16,000 enquiries and completing about 6,500 cases a year. NFM states that its aims and objectives are as follows:

> The primary aim of family mediation is to help couples involved in the process of separation and divorce to reach agreements or reduce the area or intensity of conflict between them, especially in disputes concerning children.

The NFM also defines the process of family mediation as:

> National Family Mediation defines mediation as a form of intervention involving a process in which a third party, the mediator, assists the parties in a dispute to negotiate over the issues that divide them. The mediator has no stake in the dispute and is not identified with any of the competing interests involved. The mediator has no power to impose a settlement on the parties who retain authority for making their own decisions. The mediator is therefore responsible for the conduct of the process (which is held to be discrete and unambiguous) while the parties control the outcome. [2]

NFM is committed to offering mediation on a not-for-profit basis and charges clients subsidised rates according to their means. NFM has a leading edge in quality in the provision of family mediation and is confident that once the relevant provisions of the Family Law Act 1996

---

[2] National Family Mediation *Annual Report 1996*, p. 6

are implemented, its services will meet the needs of a substantial proportion of the 40 per cent of divorcing couples who are likely to opt for mediation after the compulsory initial information meeting.

All Issues Mediation

While most local services focus on resolving disputes around the future of children, a limited number of services, including one in the West Midlands, are 'able to offer 'All Issues Mediation' which includes detailed discussion of property and finance as well as concerns directly related to the children.' All Issues Mediation was piloted in five NFM mediation services and evaluated in 1994 by the Centre for Family Studies at Newcastle University. This evaluation together with a second research report in 1996 on the longer term impact of family mediation shows that All Issues Mediation improves communication between couples, reduces bitterness and tension and achieves agreements which are more likely to survive the test of time. All Issues Mediation is available both to couples with children and to those who do not have children or whose children are no longer living at home. Family mediation services are low cost to clients, and may become eligible for legal aid.

Training of mediators

The establishment of the United Kingdom College of Family Mediators as the professional body to oversee standards of ethics and the training of family mediators is described in *Chapter 12.*

Family mediation—links with probation services

Three quarters of family mediation services function in partnership with the probation service (which has certain statutory responsibilities to provide a Family Court Welfare Service) as a major focus of the requirement of probation services to use five per cent of their budgets on joint work with the independent sector. An example of such a partnership is illustrated by the questionnaire response from a London bureau. Family mediation as an alternative to the adversarial process in court in cases of custody of and access to children was started by the South East London Probation Service in 1979. In 1995, family mediation work became a separate and independent but partner organization, the Family Mediation Bureau. This reorganization was in preparation for the implementation of the Family Law Act which requires the Family Mediation Bureau to be audited under Legal Aid Board quality assurance procedures. In addition to mediation in child related issues, the Bureau plans to recruit a family mediator who will be trained to provide All Issues Mediation.

Bureau mediators are in attendance at local family proceedings courts and are often able to assist communication and understanding between parties about the ways in which contact between children and their relatives can be arranged. The partnership between the Probation Service and the Family Mediation Bureau co-ordinates a wide range of services for families, as explained in a report from the senior court welfare officer for South-east London to the Annual General Meeting of the Bureau in 1996:

> The range of services provided to families in S E London by the two organizations is impressive. Mediation, counseling, contact centres, assistance and advice at court and the preparation of court welfare reports all help towards reducing the harm done to children through the process of separation and divorce . . . The Family Law Act will provide us with further opportunities for working together. We are well placed to put ourselves forward, working with a number of other professional disciplines, to provide information sessions for parents embarking on separation or divorce. The involvement of children in mediation may well demand collaboration between mediators and court welfare officers. Further scope for in-court mediation will be explored.

Out of a total of 268 joint mediation meetings arranged between parties by the bureau in 1995, full agreement was reached in 110 cases, part agreement in 101 cases and no agreement in only 57 cases.

The Family Mediation Bureau works closely with the local community mediation service. 'Although the respective mediation services are functioning in different fields of conflict resolution, the good rapport which has been established should help promote the concept of mediation as a means of helping people in S E London to live in greater harmony.'

There are other examples of probation services involved in family mediation, sometimes in partnership with a local voluntary service. For example, a Midlands probation service described a partnership agreement with the local family mediation service for the provision of out-of-court conciliation services. Another in the south-west offers 'court-based family mediation in private law cases.' Another probation service in the same region also offers mediation within the family courts for parents who have started court proceedings to resolve a dispute about arrangements for their children. The court welfare officer acts as mediator and the court is informed only that mediation took place but not given details of any agreement. A similar service is offered by family court welfare staff in a probation service in the north-west.

THE FAMILY MEDIATORS' ASSOCIATION

Members of the Family Mediators' Association (FMA) are lawyer mediators and family mediators in private practice who specialise in working with couples involved in separation and divorce. The FMA offers a dual model of mediation in which two mediators work together, one a solicitor mediator and the other a family mediator usually from a social work or counselling background. The solicitor mediator provides the knowledge and expertise in areas covered by the law while the family mediator uses specialist skills to facilitate a discussion which may often be charged with painful emotion. Single mediator sessions may be appropriate for some clients for whom settlement is more amicable, though the availability of a lawyer both to give information and to act as a consultant to the mediator is seen as essential. All FMA mediators, whether lawyers or not, are qualified to undertake comprehensive or All Issues Mediation. In 1992, FMA services dealt with about 1,500 cases. The FMA is a co-founder of the UK College of Family Mediators (see page 149)

Some FMA services responded to the questionnaire: for example, one from the West of England offers both Sole Mediation with one mediator working with both parties to resolve disputes relating to divorce or separation and child issues, and Comprehensive Mediation with two mediators, one being a qualified solicitor, working together with both parties to resolve All Issues disputes including property and finance. The charges are £60 per hour per couple for one mediator or £120 per hour per couple for two. Another private practice has set up in London to combine the experience and specialisation of three family law solicitors and two mediators:

> We are convinced that the time is right to create a new style of law practice, preserving (and enhancing) the best qualities of lawyers' services but drawing on the skills of co-professionals and the opportunities that now exist for starting a niche practice.

SOLICITORS' FAMILY LAW ASSOCIATION

The Solicitors' Family Law Association (SFLA) is an association of 3,500 solicitors working in family cases. Some family law solicitors are already viewing mediation as an integral part of the procedures available to separating and divorcing couples. Some are bringing family mediators into their practices while others are themselves undertaking training in mediation skills. The SFLA explains its perspective as follows:

The SFLA model follows the principles of established mediation practice while recognising that parties negotiate 'in the shadow of the law'. Its theoretical perspective may be summarised as comprising a structured, comprehensive framework bounded by a body of ethical and practice rules and clearly defined stages, within which it allows for creativity and flexibility appropriate to the parties needs and issues. It views mediation as an integral part of the system within which the parties function, standing alongside other relevant processes, including the legal process, counselling and therapy.

The training programme offered by the SFLA is described in *Chapter 12*.

ISSUES OF IMPLEMENTATION

After the Family Law Act 1996 comes into force, if the predicted 40 per cent of couples opt for mediation and the divorce rate stays constant, as many as 60,000 couples each year will be seeking mediation services.

Franchising and practice standards
The Legal Aid Board will franchise, and audit, any mediation service which reaches its standard for providers; however the government has made it clear that mediators must regulate their own standards. Unlike solicitors, the effects of whose work is visible in the public arena of the courtroom, mediators are working privately and confidentially with their clients with little oversight. The need to have in place a credible supervisory and regulatory system for mediation is an issue which has been addressed by NFM and the UK College of Family Mediators. The SFLA also recognises that 'solicitors who wish to mediate need to undergo appropriate training and to be subject to a regime involving consultancy (rather than supervision as such), accreditation and regulation.' It seems crucial that the family mediation services should develop in a coherent way so that within a free market of options to meet a variety of needs, couples facing critical personal issues at a highly emotional and painful time can be assured that they receive the same level of quality service from whatever service they choose. Discussions between the Law Society representing family solicitors who wish to mediate and the UK College of Family Mediators may result in the agreement of a common code of practice for all practising family mediators.

Women's interests
Another issue which has been the subject of debate is the possible damage of divorce mediation to women's interests. For example, Marian Roberts reviewed the facts and fears of the issue in *Family*

Mediation, the journal of the NFM. More than a decade ago, it was argued that mediation could be disadvantageous to women because of the fundamental power inequalities in the family which can be masked and perpetuated by a consensus agreement. These fears have been raised again in relation to the Family Law Act.

> They (women) are more likely in this situation to be inarticulate and ill-informed about their rights, more likely to be timid, suffering from depression and possibly in fear of their husbands. Women mediators, it is said (and most of them are women), are more likely to side with the husband's account of affairs than the wife's. The husband is more likely to be able to afford legal advice in the background, to have some experience of negotiation and to know his rights. Most seriously of all, it is not the job of the mediator, who may have no legal training at all, to inform the couple of their rights under the law.[3]

Marian Roberts challenges Deech's critique of mediation as an oversimplification of issues that are 'complex, multifaceted and interdependent.' She points out that 'Rarely are the disadvantages or advantages stacked all one way, nor should it be assumed that, where one party has superior 'endowments' of one sort or another, that power will necessarily be used, let alone exploited.' She defends mediation as a way of redressing power imbalances in a conflict situation but expectations that it is a complete remedy for the ills of society are unrealistic. This is clearly a debate that is likely to continue. The benefits of mediation both to women and to men need continued evaluation. Mediation does not create a new world; it can only attempt to use the best possible strategies to arrange existing building blocks into an acceptable structure for all concerned.

MEDIATION IN FAMILY DISPUTES

Family mediation is also helpful in family disputes which do not involve divorce or separation settlements. Mediation as well as other forms of conflict resolution can be and are used to improve and strengthen relationships within families. A wide range of agencies and organizations see family mediation as *part of* their activity. Within the voluntary sector, responses to the questionnaire (*Chapter 3*) included eight examples of community mediation services offering mediation in conflicts which arise from family disputes.

The Post-Adoption Centre Mediation Service is a research project set up to evaluate the use of mediation in negotiating contact

---

[3] Deech 1995, p.12

arrangements between natural parents (sometimes called birth parents) and adoptive parents. The adoption process is long and complicated and charged with emotion for the parties, involving a network of professional agencies and formal court proceedings. The aim of the project is to provide at all stages of the process an independent and neutral mediator to help both sets of parents to understand what is happening, reduce dispute between them and agree arrangements about future contact that will be in the best interests of the child. The coordinator of the project writes:

> I would argue that, from different perspectives, the birth parent and the adoptive parents come to mediation feeling disempowered and unentitled. The process of empowerment and entitlement is inextricably bound up in the symbolic relationship between the two parties—the birth parent needs to have her place in the child's life validated by the adoptive parent; and the adoptive parent needs to feel entitled to become the parent of this child. Can mediation as a process in and of itself create the environment in which this mutuality can be expressed and explored?

The co-ordinator discusses the difficulties that arise from the highly charged emotions that the situation evokes and the lack of professional consensus about what are the best interests of the child. There are also question marks about the neutrality of the mediators who have the dual role of post-adoption counsellors at the centre. Nevertheless the coordinator is optimistically convinced that an independent mediation service can be of enormous benefit to both sets of parents 'in transforming the adversarial and paternalistic adoption culture into one where co-operation and mutuality are prioritised'.

The Elder Mediation Project
Another exciting pilot project is the Elder Mediation Project (EMP). A multi-cultural group of older volunteers aiming to help other older people to cope constructively with later life conflicts. These may be conflicts within the family, with neighbours (see also page 56) or involving those living in residential care. Older people often feel disempowered and discriminated against merely on the ground of age and sometimes because of disability. The project's volunteers are committed to working with older people to enable them to have an equal voice in the settlement of later life conflicts in an appropriate way.

Teen/parent mediation
Teen/parent mediation has developed as a distinctive category in Canada in response to the needs of a growing number of parents who feel that their relationship with their teenage children is breaking down.

The mediation process is effective in enabling parents and their children to listen and understand each others' points of view and to work out ground rules which allow mutual acceptance of freedoms, rights and responsibilities. A worker who has experience of teen/parent mediation comments that problems can arise if the teenagers feel that they cannot trust the impartiality of an adult mediator.

Domestic violence

Mediators in family conflicts have to be sensitive to the possibility that domestic violence may be part of the problem. While most mediation services do not feel that disputes in which domestic violence is present can be mediated, a response from a mediation service in the south-west gave domestic violence as one of its fields of activity. This voluntary service has worked closely with local police to develop the option of mediation in domestic violence cases. The coordinator in question stressed that only professionally qualified staff work with domestic violence cases, which require skills beyond those held by most volunteer community mediators.

FAMILY GROUP CONFERENCES

An example of local authority social services involvement in family mediation comes from an authority in the south of the country where family group conferences (FGCs) are being piloted as a different method of working with families. This model of family-decision making stems from New Zealand and the traditional ways of the Maori community. It is being tried in a UK setting for three years during which it will be monitored and evaluated by a team from the local university. The process of Family Group Conferences brings together significant family members with professionals to share knowledge and ideas about the future well-being of the child or children of the family. Once the professionals have shared their knowledge and views with the family members, the family is left alone, or with a facilitator if members prefer, to work out a plan which is accepted by the professionals unless it is perceived as harmful to the child.

FGCs—which used as a way of empowering families to resolve conflict in a cooperative way and to plan for the future—have been found so far to have very positive outcomes. They are not offering a mediation process but are a way of enabling families to resolve conflicts of interests in a non-confrontational way both within the family group and vis-à-vis the professionals involved. The project is a demonstration of the possibilities of innovative ADR approaches. FGCs are also being used to deal with young offenders: see p. 72.

CONCLUSION

This chapter has reviewed the field of family mediation and looked at the development of two strands of family mediation arising from the massive increase in the divorce rate since 1971. The work of National Family Mediation and its network of Family Mediation Services has developed in the voluntary sector in response to the needs of families in crisis. Legal interest in the processes of mediation through the work of the Solicitors' Family Law Association and the Family Mediators' Association has grown in answer to the requirements of the Family Law Act 1996. How can the part to be played by both types of service within the new legal framework best be structured and clarified to meet the increasing demands and pressures from clients?

However, mediation within families in conflict is not always associated with divorce. A range of statutory and voluntary agencies is exploring strategies for enabling families in situations which are highly charged with emotion to resolve conflict cooperatively and creatively. The main thrust of many innovative projects is to enable families to reclaim decision-making about their lives from professionals. Within professional agencies where intervention is required, there are opportunities, in the probation services, social services and the police, for the development of ADR strategies as part of their response to, for example, child abuse and domestic violence. Given creative thinking and funding for research and pilot schemes, might such projects also satisfy the search for cost-effectiveness and efficiency?

SOURCES AND FURTHER READING: *Chapter 4*

Ahier, B., *Conciliation, Divorce and the Probation Service*, 1986
Craig, Y., 'Ageism: Cases and Concerns', *Mediation*, Vol. 11:3, Summer 1995, p. 12; and 'The Ability to Mediate', *Mediation*, Vol. 11: 4, Autumn 1995, p. 12
Dingwall R., and Eekelaar J., *Divorce Mediation and the Legal Process*, 1988
Family Law Act 1996
Friedman, G., *A Guide to Divorce Mediation: How to Reach a Fair Legal Settlement at A Fraction of the Cost*, 1993
Lupton, C., Barnard, S., and Swall-Yarrington, M., *Family Planning?: An Evaluation of the Family Group Conference Model*, University of Portsmouth Social Services Research and Information Unit, 1995
Mediation: The Making and Remaking of Cooperative Relationships: An Evaluation of the Effectiveness of Comprehensive Mediation, University of Newcastle, 1994
Roberts, M., *Mediation in Family Disputes: A Guide to Practice*, 1988
Looking Into The Future: Mediation and the Ground for Divorce, Green Paper, Lord Chancellor's Department, 1993, Cmnd. 2799, p. 72
Roberts, M., 'Family Mediation and the Interests of Women', *Family Law*, Vol. 26, April 1996, pp. 239-241; and *Family Mediation*, Vol. 6:2, August 1996, p.8

Sales, S., 'Mediation in Adoption: Some Reflections on a New Service', *Family Mediation*, Vol. 6:1, Spring 1996

The Longer-Term Impact of Family Mediation, University of Newcastle, 1996.

Ackowledgments
Thelma Fisher, National Family Mediation
Sally Sales
Yvonne Craig
Family Mediation Association
Solicitors' Family Law Association
Coventry and Warwickshire Family Mediation Service
South East London Family Mediation Bureau
Post-Adoption Centre Mediation Service
Elder Mediation Project
University of Portsmouth Social Services Research and Information Unit
Hampshire Social Services
Warwickshire Probation Service
Avon Probation Service
Gloucester Probation Service (Family Courts Service)
Greater Manchester Probation Service
ACCORD, Cornwall
Family Law Consortium, London WC2.

CHAPTER 5

Mediation Between Neighbours

A number of organizations, including Mediation UK and schemes run by
local authorities, provide mediation services which are designed primarily
to resolve disputes between neighbours. These have made a considerable
contribution to the resolution of disputes, resulting in a significant saving
to the court system. . . . they may offer a better, a less confrontational way
of dealing with disputes between neighbours where a continuing
relationship is important.

Lord Woolf, Access to Justice, The Final Report, 1996

Mediation as a way of resolving neighbour disputes is perhaps the most
publicised field of recent growth in the management of conflict. In this
chapter the current causes and context of neighbour disputes are
discussed. Evidence of multi-disciplinary approaches and links between
neighbour mediation and other developing fields of conflict resolution
is also reviewed. Issues of concern about the future of neighbour
mediation are also outlined.

CONFLICT BETWEEN NEIGHBOURS

Research into the current causes of neighbour disputes has concentrated
on the presenting triggers rather than underlying situations. Many
conflicts involve noise from dogs, loud music, children and DIY work.
Similarly, car parking, overhanging trees and rubbish are cited as other
sources of dispute. A survey conducted in 1991 and published in 1996
by the Department of the Environment on attitudes to noise found that
noisy neighbours were the third most frequently noticed source of
disturbing noise. A neighbour dispute survey made during 1994 by
researchers from the Centre for Criminological and Legal Research at
Sheffield University found that 62 per cent of complaints to
environmental health officers involved domestic noise. This was
followed—a long way behind—by nuisance from dogs, and in gardens
and common areas. A sample of eleven housing departments provided
the researchers with information indicating that two-fifths of neighbour
nuisance complaints involved noise, with property abuse and personal
conflict also scoring significantly.

Examples from the information provided in responses to the
questionnaire (*Chapter 3*) illustrate that the pattern of causes found by

the Sheffield researchers is reflected, with some local variation due to different methods of categorisation, in disputes brought to local mediation services in different parts of the UK, as shown in *Table 5.1.*

	South London med. service 150 cases	East Anglia med. service 71 cases/164 causes	Scottish med. service 210 cases	Yorkshire service 105 cases
Noise	54%	27%	41%	38%
Aggressive/anti-social behaviour	18%	16%	12%	17%
Damage or invasion of property	6%	20%	10%	18%
Children/young people	4.5%	6%	2%	16%
Animals		4.4%	6%	2%
Misc/unspecified	11%	23%	5%	11%

Table 5.1: Causes of Neighbour Disputes

Cases resulting from conflict between neighbours highlight how apparently insignificant sources of disagreement can escalate into long and costly confrontational battles, sometimes with tragic consequences. A dispute over a row of conifers which cost two neighbours legal fees of over £100,000 may seem absurd, but the long-running hostility between two families which, in 1996, ended in the beating to death of a young man in his front garden demonstrates an extreme, albeit rare, outcome of a dispute.

An increasing phenomena
The incidence and seriousness of neighbour disputes are perceived by communities to be increasing. Community workers on a West London high-rise estate in the 1980s were told of a 'golden age' before all the little streets of mean terraced housing were pulled down to make way for the new estate. It was said that in those days people were all good neighbours: everyone was poor and no one had anything worth stealing; all doors were left unlocked and children treated all houses as their own homes. Now people locked and barred their doors, fearing for their videos and stereos and even their lives; the elderly feared to walk the streets because of muggers, and children were kept in their own homes away from trouble. A culture of co-operation, remembered in the rosy glow of hindsight, had changed into a culture of competition and

confrontation, leading to envy and fear. Where formerly a bit of neighbourly noise had been tolerated with give-and-take and disputes were settled on the spot by the natural leaders in the street, now the beat from the stereo next door was an invasion of space which triggered resentment and provided a flash-point for conflict. High density living in blocks of flats and closely built housing developments made neighbour disputes more likely and proximity, areas of common use such as staircases, lifts and walkways and poor sound insulation in party walls create conditions which exacerbate mutual irritation and turn disagreements into disputes.

The nostalgic recollections of the older inhabitants of this area and their present-day fears and tensions could be replicated, with variations, thousands of times across the country and perhaps begin to suggest some of the questions that should be asked about the social and economic causes of the current rise in concern about neighbour conflict, though neighbour disputes happen in affluent suburbs and rural areas as well as in cities. A National Good Neighbours Survey by the General Accident insurance company in 1995 examined the attitude of people towards their neighbours and found that 20 per cent of the sample admitted to having quarrelled with their neighbours, seven per cent claimed to have reported a neighbour to the police and six per cent to the environmental health department.

Politicians in rare cross-party consensus have reacted to perceived public concern with a series of confrontational proposals including eviction of public housing tenants who are judged to be persistently 'troublesome' and jail sentences for neighbours who threaten violence or are responsible for frequent noise disturbance. Curfews have been suggested as a means of curbing aggression and the use of private detectives to collect evidence to present in court is proposed as a way round the fear of reprisal for speaking out. These proposals do not provide solutions to the problems arising from neighbour conflict and contribute to an increase in community tension rather than to creative efforts to resolve the causes of conflict.

DEVELOPMENT OF MEDIATION SERVICES

Mediation has been developed by local voluntary groups as an alternative, non-confrontational way of resolving disputes and improving community harmony. The first neighbour mediation service began work in 1982 in East London and neighbour mediation was one of the three main strands of alternative dispute resolution work developed by the Forum for Initiatives in Reparation and Mediation (FIRM) from 1983. Since then, voluntary groups dedicated to challenging both the increase in neighbour disputes and confrontational approaches to dealing with them have responded by forming neighbour mediation services under the umbrella of FIRM, which in 1991 became Mediation UK, the 'network of projects, organizations and individuals interested in mediation and other constructive forms of conflict resolution'. In the Mediation UK 1996 Directory, 76 accredited local member groups are listed as well as many other interested and relevant organizations and agencies. New groups are being formed even as this is being written. Mediation UK through its research, publications and annual conferences has become the driving force behind the growth of voluntary neighbour mediation services.

Nature of neighbour mediation services

The response from neighbour mediation services to the questionnaire (*Chapter 3*) was very high, giving substantial insights into the nature of these groups. Seventy organizations responded giving neighbour mediation as a field of activity, 37 of them specialising in that field, while a further 18 community mediation services offer neighbour mediation as one of their fields. Fifteen organizations, including housing associations, local housing departments and police forces, offered neighbour mediation as a service peripheral to their main purpose. The responses were drawn from all parts of the British Isles.

North 10	Scotland 2	Wales 3	
South-west 6	Midlands 15	East Anglia 4	
London 15	South-east 12	Northern Ireland 1	Irish Republic 2

Table 5.2: Responses by Region

Eight of the organizations were in the early stages of formation with involvement of steering groups, consultants and trainers, perhaps an average of ten people per group. Numbers of staff and volunteers involved in 62 actively working groups illustrate the crucial part played by volunteers in the field; 87 full-time and part-time workers are supported and helped by 788 volunteer mediators, a ratio of 1:9.

The groups which were already diversifying into other fields of mediation demonstrated that they respond to a wide range of needs: group facilitation (3), schools (5), peer mediation (youth) (3), family (11), workplace (2), victim/offender (4), domestic violence (1), complaints (2). Their activities in these fields will be discussed in the appropriate sections.

46

The groups put high priority on training their mediators and 49 organizations ran their own training schemes. (Discussion of the issues concerning the training of mediators is reserved for *Chapter 12*). They are formed either by dedicated local individuals or by coalitions of other interests in the community, both voluntary and statutory, or by a combination of these. Once formed, groups quickly establish links with other agencies in order to promote their work and these develop over time to form solid networks of contacts and referral agencies so that their services become widely known and available to those who might need them. Links most frequently mentioned by groups are:

Statutory	Voluntary
Local authorities	Mediation UK
Local housing departments	Society of Friends
Local environmental departments	Local churches
Local health authorities	Housing associations
Local social services	Citizens Advice Bureaux
Police	Council of Voluntary Service
Probation services	Tenants-residents associations
Safer Cities	Local victim-offender groups
Schools	Victim Support schemes
Local universities	Local law centres

Table 5.3: Links Established by Neighbourhood Mediation Groups

The groups receive funding from a variety of statutory and charitable sources, but often their budgets are insecure and the work of applying each year for renewal of grants or money from new sources diverts valuable time and energy away from mediating disputes. Some voluntary neighbour mediation services are expanding their funding, and therefore their scope, by taking fees for service contracts (discussed on page 000). However, to the clients seeking mediation in their disputes, the service is free. This is an important part of their ethos, closely linked with their commitment to voluntary, community-based teams of mediators

In addition to the proliferating voluntary mediation services, there are some being developed from initiatives by local authorities. A small number of private organizations are now offering neighbour mediation; such profit-making organizations charge for the services of a mediator. Their rates, depending on the time spent on a case, work out in the region of £250 plus VAT and expenses.

Most groups and many individuals become members of Mediation UK, which serves 'individuals and projects involved or interested in constructive ways of settling conflicts', and offers a network of training and support services.

Publicity and annual reports

Mediation services explain their role and availability to their communities by leaflets and posters distributed and displayed in places where potential clients might see them such as post offices, doctors' surgeries, libraries and churches. A typical leaflet advertising the work of a mediation service explains the process and emphasises, very clearly, the benefits on offer. The ethical framework of independence, confidentiality and impartiality expressed in publicity material and annual reports is common to all members of Mediation UK and is shared by all the groups which responded to the questionnaire. A comprehensive statement of the aims, claims and scope of a service is given in the annual report of a Scottish service:

MEDIATION is a process in which someone neutral helps people in dispute to reach agreement. It helps people identify what they want to happen, and how everyone can act to stop the conflict.

MEDIATION concentrates on how people will act towards each other in the future, not what has happened in the past.

MEDIATION aims to bring people together, not make their differences greater.

MEDIATION builds on people's common sense, and does not depend on difficult legal arguments and case-law.

MEDIATION helps people involved in a dispute to find the solution themselves, not have an outside solution forced on them by someone who doesn't really know what they want or need.

MEDIATION looks for a solution in which everyone is better off, not just whoever 'won' their case.

MEDIATION is cheap and fast compared with other ways of resolving disputes.

MEDIATION is tried and tested and has a good track-record.

EFFECTIVENESS OF MEDIATION

Naturally, for a mediation service to flourish it is helpful for it to gain a reputation for success in its work. Case studies demonstrate how effective mediation can dramatically improve the quality of life for individuals and communities. A typical case, with some details changed to protect confidentiality, illustrates how mediation works:

> Mr and Mrs Jones are a young couple in their mid-twenties with two young children. Mrs Smith, their next door neighbour, is a recently widowed woman in her mid-sixties, now living alone.
>
> The dispute rose over noise nuisance, which was a result of Mrs Smith leaving her radio on whilst she was out of the house. This extended to leaving the radio on 24 hours a day when she would stay with relatives some weekends.
>
> Mr and Mrs Jones were finding the noise disturbing especially for one of their children who had recently undergone surgery following a long illness. His sleep and rest during the day and early evening were being disturbed by the constant playing of the radio next door.
>
> Mrs Jones had approached her neighbour about the problem but no satisfactory solution had been reached. Both parties agreed to mediation and several visits were made to each party by the mediator culminating in a face-to-face meeting. During the face-to-face meeting Mrs Jones was able to inform her neighbour of her son's illness and treatment. She explained how the noise was affecting the family.
>
> Mrs Smith was able to explain that since she had become widowed she had a fear of entering a silent house and more so a fear of finding her house had been burgled. She left her radio on to give the impression that someone was at home; it also meant that she did not have to enter a silent house. After listening to her neighbour, for the first time Mrs Smith accepted how her behaviour was affecting the Jones family. She went on to say that her family had insisted she had a burglar alarm fitted following the death of her husband but she never used it for fear of it going off when she was away from home.
>
> Both parties agreed that in future, rather than leave the radio on, Mrs Smith would set her alarm, informing Mrs Jones of her whereabouts and giving a contact number. The meeting ended with Mrs Smith offering a full apology for the distress she had caused to the Jones family. Both parties left on good terms. Follow-up contact six months after the face-to-face meeting reported that both parties were enjoying a good relationship.

This case illustrates both the simplicity and the complexity of neighbour disputes. The cause is apparently simple—the intrusion of noise from one neighbour invading the space of the other. But lack of effective communication and therefore understanding between the two neighbours turned a simple inconvenience into the grounds for a dispute. Mediation, the intervention of the neutral third party, enabled the neighbours to communicate their needs and emotions and to understand each other's problems. New understanding and compromise was reached and a sound basis for the development of a closer and happier future relationship was secured.

Mediators know from experience that while some cases will reach successful resolution, others will present complex problems and in the end mediation may prove impractical. Reported success rates vary. In the South London mediation service, 44 per cent of cases taken in the year 1995-6 reached a resolution or succeeded in bringing about improvement in a neighbour relationship. A Scottish project reported that it 'either resolved the dispute or considerably improved relationships in well over 50 per cent of cases that got beyond the initial stage, using methods ranging from face-to-face meetings and shuttle diplomacy'. The Neighbour Disputes survey from Sheffield University made an analysis of reported outcomes in the services under study which showed that nearly a quarter of mediations achieved complete agreement and a further third succeeded in improving relationships between the parties in dispute.

For a case to proceed to successful mediation, *both* parties have to agree to take part and it is clear from the evidence that this is the crucial hurdle. 48 per cent of cases referred to the South London mediation service failed because one party or the other either withdrew, declined to take part or would not even establish contact. Out of the 68 East Anglian cases, 52 could not proceed because one or other of the parties refused contact or withdrew. Once that hurdle is passed, the success rate of mediation in resolving or at the least ameliorating disputes is high. This demonstrates the great need for awareness-raising about the nature of the mediation process and the benefits of successful mediation. An article in *The Guardian* (26 November 1996) suggested that mediation services only tackled a fraction of the need:

> Local officers may recommend mediation, but people prepared to go to voluntary mediation are probably already prepared to settle. Mediation UK [reports] a 34 per cent increase in enquiries last year. Even so, they [mediation services] only dealt with around 2,000 cases — set against 200,000 complaints to local authority about neighbourhood noise.

Some referrals fail to proceed to mediation because the dispute, on examination, is assessed to be unsuited to this process. These are generally cases where one of the parties is involved in criminal activity or already undergoing criminal investigation. The Sheffield research recommended more effective targeting of cases where mediation is most likely to succeed and suggested a set of criteria which at an early stage could screen out those cases which are inappropriate for referral to mediation. Such targeting would increase the cost-effectiveness of mediation in neighbour disputes. Although the report highlights the difficulties in calculating costs and the need for more research, nevertheless the findings encouraged the researchers to conclude that:

> Given the ineffectiveness of existing approaches to many problems involving disputes between neighbours, we believe that there is a case for extending the use of mediation, particularly if ways can be found for 'targeting' it on those cases where the prospects for success (and the scope for significant reductions in the human, social and financial costs involved) are greatest.

EXAMPLES OF MEDIATION SERVICES

Some profiles of typical neighbour mediation services serve to illustrate the variety of approaches in this field.

South London
The South London service whose case load has already been quoted was set up in 1990. There are currently 23 active volunteers and only in the Autumn of 1996 did the organization move from a base in the home of two of the founder members into office accommodation. The total expenditure of this service in 1995-6 was fractionally over £3,000; in 1997 this was set to rise to just over £4,000, and it is hoped that it may be possible to employ a part-time co-ordinator.

A service in the south-west
A neighbour mediation service in the south-west was set up as a voluntary organization in 1992 with funding from the local authority, the Home Office ('Safer Cities') and the local health authority. While the core work of the service provided by volunteers was in neighbour mediation, it received sufficient funds to employ five full time staff and three part-time staff, four and two of them respectively engaged in case work and the rest providing administrative support. The staff have counselling and family mediation skills and initially developed work in the field of victim-offender mediation, until support from the local probation service was withdrawn through problems with funding. Since 1994 they have specialised in mediation in cases of domestic violence which are mediated by staff with appropriate professional qualifications. The 25 volunteer mediators were trained in-house in community mediation skills which the co-ordinator identified as a 'niche version' of broad mediation skills. Around 250 neighbour dispute referrals are received per year of which about 150 are actively pursued. The average time spent per case is eight hours and the outcomes are split three ways: a third are resolved, a third are 'sort of

resolved and a third do not result in a successful resolution of the dispute. The co-ordinator identified the most urgent need of the service as the expansion of funding so that more staff could be employed to increase the specialist side of the organization's work.

East Anglia

The East Anglian service was set up in 1993 and by 1995-6 had a budget of about £6,000 made up of grants from three local authorities. The chairperson in her annual report explained the reluctance to employ staff:

> We have talked about employing staff for some time and had some hesitations because of the perception we had of the value of an all-volunteer service. But during the summer we realised that our volunteers were being overstretched and that this was not effective.

The decision was taken to employ a part-time administrator to support the work of the 20 active volunteers.

Yorkshire

A Yorkshire group was set up in 1988 but has been externally funded only since 1995 by the local housing department and Safer Cities. It employs two part-time staff and has 38 volunteers who take referrals from Housing, Environmental Health, Housing Associations, the police and Citizen's Advice Bureaux as well as self-referrals. Although grant-aided, 'the service is managed by a voluntary Management Committee and is completely independent of any statutory agency.'

Scotland

A Scottish project was established in 1995 under the management of SACRO and funded through the Urban Programme with the support of the local authority and the Scottish Office. It has a paid staff of three case workers and an administrator and 20 volunteers and reports:

> Our volunteers are working to the best professional standards, and we value them very highly. Without their talent and commitment it would be impossible for the project to attempt the volume and range of work that is currently undertaken.

This service is an example of a group in the middle ground between voluntary and statutory.

DEVELOPMENT OF SERVICES

Groups such as the ones in South London, Yorkshire and East Anglia have grown from community roots starting, often literally, with a group of concerned local people in someone's front room, and maintaining their commitment to independence even when supported by local authority finance. By contrast, the Scottish example was established as a partnership between the local authority and an established national voluntary organization and existing local community organizations with an advisory committee representing these interested bodies.

There is a small but growing number of instances of statutory authorities taking an interest, and sometimes the initiative, in setting up a mediation service in collaboration with a voluntary group. For example, in a London borough housing department a three year development plan has the objective of setting up a fully funded Independent Mediation Service.

> The intention is for the service to be very much a local initiative for the people of the borough . . . currently, a small group of people, who share a common interest in the project, is being established; the Management Committee will evolve from here. The service is being set up with a similar structure to the majority of the other mediation services that exist at present in the UK. Since the service will use volunteer mediators, the recruitment process of these volunteers will have begun by the anticipated start date of the co-ordinator. . . . The coordinator will be responsible for taking over a project, when the essential start up work will have been completed. His/her task will be to ensure that the service evolves into a financially viable and well-run service for the borough.

In another London borough, a probation worker has been seconded part-time to the local housing department as community safety co-ordinator to investigate the feasibility of setting up a mediation service, in the first instance for tenants of local authority housing. This initiative is strongly supported by the community liaison officer from the local police force as there is a high level of concern about the increasing demands on police time because of call-outs to neighbour disputes. The police borough liaison officer explained that police have neither the time nor the training to act as mediators. Nor are they perceived as impartial with the result that after giving their best efforts, some disputants make complaints against them which required more time to investigate. The intention is to set up an independent volunteer-led service through development of interest within existing tenants' and residents' associations.

Police in a southern county recognised that their role includes time-consuming neighbour mediation, though their powers in relation to 'nuisance' type offences are often limited. They propose to liaise with other organizations, public and private, to reduce the incidence of neighbourhood nuisance and dispute. Among the examples of good practice they cite collaboration with mediation and in particular voluntary mediation services set up under the Mediation UK umbrella as an appropriate strategy.

INFLUENCE OF THE CONTRACT CULTURE

At the present time, the majority of neighbour mediation services are community based, voluntary organizations. Many people trust them for their standards of impartiality, confidentiality and independence and find them more accessible than, for example, a local authority office. As more mediation services are set up through initiative from statutory authorities, and voluntary mediation services rely increasingly heavily on local authority grants for staffing costs, issues around the public's perception of their impartiality and independence may be raised. Mediation services need good relations with statutory agencies so that cases suitable for mediation are swiftly referred to them. There are examples among the respondents of community mediation services seeking out and committing themselves to a new kind of relationship in the form of service contracts with local housing departments, health authorities and housing associations. Under these contracts, the mediation service undertakes to accept a certain number of referrals in a year from the agency for a fixed payment, with additional fees for cases in excess of that number.

Apart from public authorities, housing associations are the most common organizations with which mediation services make service contracts. A sample of 85 Housing Associations was sent questionnaires of which 13 responded (15 per cent). Of these, four had no mechanism for dealing with disputes and five had procedures in place for dealing with the complaints and grievances of their tenants. The remaining four included neighbour mediation as a small part of their activity or indicated that they had a procedure for referring disputes to the local mediation service. From the sample of 60 mediation services, eleven mentioned significant links with housing associations, either as providers of support, as agencies making referrals or organizations with which formal service links have been established.

Risks
Although service contracts offer the advantage of secure funding and may enable expansion, there are also risks involved in such dependence. For example, the practice may call in question the independence of the mediation service. Organizations which undertake contract work are under pressure to fulfil their commitments which may skew their take-up of cases and leave them less freedom to give

prompt and effective service to self-referrals and referrals from agencies outside the contractual arrangements. Because of the requirement to fulfil a contract, paid staff whose availability can be guaranteed may be assigned to cases in preference to volunteers, which could contribute to the growth of a 'professional' service in which volunteers play a supporting rather than a central role. The agencies may be seeking to save money by contracting out dispute resolution work. They will require reports, monitoring of caseloads, outcomes and costs, creating more administrative work for mediation services leading to the development of bureaucratic systems which may begin to stultify the creative freedom of community mediation.

LINKS WITH OTHER DEVELOPING FIELDS

The interest of local police forces in voluntary sector neighbour mediation services highlights the way in which neighbourhood work can lead to victim-offender mediation. Amongst the respondents, three police forces and six neighbour mediation services indicated both neighbour and victim-offender as fields of activity and these form two of the three main areas of work coordinated by Mediation UK. The co-ordinator of a Scottish mediation service, which currently offers mediation only in neighbour disputes, is aware that sometimes a neighbour dispute involves inequalities of power between one party who is a victim and the other who is the offender. Sometimes such a dispute will escalate into violence and involve police intervention, criminal prosecution and needs the skills and knowledge of a victim-offender mediator. The co-ordinator offered the following case study as a recent example illustrating these issues:

A couple with three daughters, the eldest aged 17, lived in the upper part of a council house. A woman lives with her 25 year old son downstairs. She has had one serious operation and faces another shortly. She is very distressed about this situation.

Her son has recently been released from a six month prison sentence for an underage sex conviction. The eldest girl of the upstairs couple has also had sex with the son; although she had given her consent, she felt 'she had been talked into it'. When the girl's parents found out about the relationship between their daughter and the young man and about his previous conviction, they were furious. The father said he would kill the young man if he came near the house and he assaulted him on one occasion when there were no witnesses. The young man did not press charges as 'he did not want trouble'. His wish was simply to return to take care of his mother before her next operation.

Mediation was approached by the young man's mother who was desperate to have her son move back home. Mediators visited both parties, although the young man had to visit the office for the meeting as he could not go home. The father was willing to allow a two hour daily visit only because he felt sorry for the sick mother and understood both the gravity of her condition and her desire to have her visit, but he could not tolerate longer than two hours for a visit.

The agreement reached was for a two hour daily morning visit and guaranteed safe arrival and departure. It also ensured that the young man respected the time exactly and did not push, even by a few minutes in either direction.

Mediators also arranged home help and put in motion a request for immediate housing transfer. Because of the serious nature of the case and the agreement made, Police were notified.

The case is significant for mediation for several reasons, including:

- the close working relationships with police in monitoring the agreement
- the clear success of an agreement in avoiding a criminal charge, probably of a nature
- the clear success in mediation being viable in a situation involving extreme emotion.

The development of victim-offender mediation programmes is described in *Chapter 6.* Neighbour mediation work increasingly spreads and overlaps into other fields of conflict resolution activity in addition to victim-offender mediation. The benefits of raising awareness about alternative, problem-solving ways of dealing with disputes of all kinds can permeate and transform the lives of individuals and communities. Many community mediation services are becoming involved in a variety of fields and are spreading their message, as one worker said, 'like liquid gold' wherever people feel the need for a new approach to resolving conflict.

Some of the work of the Elder Mediation Project already described (see page 39) concerns the support of elderly people involved in neighbour disputes. Often disputes involve more than immediate, close neighbours and concern whole communities. There may be cross-generational elements as in the example of the work of EMP or in work with young people in the community. Thus, for example:

- a piece of community mediation involving young people and the residents of a whole street is described in *Chapter 7* (page 89)

- in many urban areas, neighbour mediation may involve cross-cultural disputes or racist behaviour. Cross-cultural mediation is discussed in *Chapter 8*
- the local focus of a community is often a school, and neighbour disputes may be taken by parents into the school environment or disputes in school, such as incidents of bullying in the playground, may spill out on to the streets. Mediation work in schools is the subject of *Chapter 7*.

CHANGING ROLE OF THE MEDIATOR?

The development of mediation services, though welcome in extending the option of mediation to more people in a variety of conflict situations, raises issues about the role of the mediator. The co-ordinator of a Scottish service, although satisfied with the outcome of the case described above, voiced concerns common to a number of respondents to the questionnaire. She finds that the service is more and more taking up advocacy, mediating with public authorities and agencies on behalf of individuals in the community, in this case in negotiations both with the police and with the local housing department on behalf of the clients. This may be perceived as a legitimate function of community mediation services and a necessary part of resolving neighbour disputes, but the coordinator is aware that acting as an advocate increases the power invested in the mediator. Instead of being a facilitator who enables disputing neighbours to identify their own solutions, the mediator becomes the problem solver and arbiter. Sally Engle Merry opened up these issues in her critique of mediation (1983):

> Despite the promise of mediation, it is important to take a hard look at what mediation really is and can really do. Many of its strengths are not those touted in its myths and many of its weaknesses are ignored. The process is not as benign or free of danger to social justice and individual liberty as its proponents would have us think. The possibility of infringing the rights of weaker parties, the potential for manipulation by mediators, the existence of subtle forms of coercion, the effects of incorporation within institutions, and the possibility of an extension of middle-class control over the working class are nagging questions cannot be ignored. Mediation can end up a new forum in which the predominantly middle-class helping professions are invited to supervise and control the private lives of the working class.

Merry's viewpoint usefully opens up questions about the ethics of mediation which are of concern to mediators in all fields and debate on the issues continues. The concerns expressed both by Merry and by the co-ordinator of a neighbour mediation service about the possibility of abuse of mediation recurs in other contexts (see p. 173).

CONCLUSION

The field of neighbour mediation explored in this chapter is one dominantly occupied by the voluntary sector with locally based, community mediation services developing in response to perceived need. A strong and supportive umbrella organization, Mediation UK, offers guidance, information, a network of contacts, annual conferences, a regular newsletter and an ethical framework which local organizations can link into and use as they require while keeping their individuality and independence. Regional support groups of local services have been formed to strengthen links between mediation services and to assist the formation of new groups. Although vigorous and expanding, mediation services can only meet the needs of those disputants willing to engage in the process.

The level of involvement of statutory agencies in neighbour mediation varies from area to area. Examples of local housing authorities initiating neighbourhood mediation services have been described. Funding needs have brought voluntary groups into closer relationships with local authorities and housing associations. Support from the police, arising from their need to have a referral point for neighbour disputes to which they are summoned has given impetus to some local services. Arising from involvement in disputes which lead to violence and crime, some neighbour mediation organizations find themselves drawn into work akin to victim-offender mediation. Sometimes they are called upon to act as advocates on behalf of clients, which may compromise the strict neutrality and impartiality that a mediator tries to preserve.

As shown by the quotation at the head of this chapter, the benefits of mediation were acknowledged in Lord Woolf's report. The use of mediation in neighbour disputes is further encouraged by the Lord Chancellor's department in a booklet about settling disputes without going to court. Encouragement from within the judicial system for an increased use of neighbour mediation emphasises the need to ask questions about the future of the service. How can it best make known the services it offers and how can it educate neighbours in dispute to seek mediation as an alternative way to resolve their conflicts? If it succeeds in becoming the accepted way for dispute resolution between neighbours, how will groups cope with the caseload? How far and for how long can it remain a service delivered primarily by volunteer mediators? Where do the boundaries lie between disputes which are capable of mediation by volunteers, however well trained they may be in mediation skills, and those which are not appropriate for resolution by mediation techniques? How can independence, impartiality and confidentiality be sustained alongside the need for funding to maintain and develop services and the growth of closer links with other agencies? How are issues of professionalism, power and class to be addressed?

While a searching debate about the future of mediation is a source of its energy, its clearly stated aspirations as a way to resolve neighbour disputes are an affirmation of its strength.

SOURCES AND FURTHER READING: *Chapter 5*

Access to Justice ('The Woolf Report'), 1996
Dignan, J., Sorsby, A. and Hibbert, J., *Neighbour Disputes: Comparing the Cost-effectiveness of Mediation and Alternative Approaches*, 1996
Kingston Friends, *Introduction to Mediation*, 1991
Lord Chancellor's Department, *Resolving Disputes Without Going to Court*, HMSO
Mediation UK, *Annual Report 1995-96*
Mediation UK, *Directory of Mediation and Conflict Resolution Services*, 1996

Acknowledgments
All the voluntary mediation services who responded to the questionnaire described in *Chapter 3*, and especially:

Mediation UK
Mediation Sheffield
Cambridge Community Mediation
Lambeth Mediation Service
Newham Conflict and Change
Edinburgh Community Mediation
Sandwell Mediation Service
Plymouth Mediation
Sneighton/St. Anns Mediation Service, Nottingham
Fife Community Mediation
Derby Mediation Service
Leeds Community Mediation
London Borough of Hounslow Housing Department
London Borough of Richmond Housing Department
Hampshire Constabulary.

CHAPTER 6

Restorative Justice

> Nobody now regards imprisonment, in itself, as an effective means of reform for most prisoners.
>
> White Paper: *Crime, Justice and Protecting the Public* (1995)

> Victim Support works for the rights of victims and their families and for greater awareness of the effects of crime.
>
> Victim Support

> Mediation offers victims and offenders the opportunity to communicate directly or indirectly through an impartial third party. The process recognises the relationship between the two parties which is largely ignored by the court process. The objectives of mediation include giving the victim a voice, making a direct impact on the offender and validating the experience of those involved in and affected by the offence.
>
> Sheffield Victim-Offender Mediation

Criminal law is the means by which a society defines the boundaries of permissible behaviour and the criminal justice process is the mechanism for administering the law. By breaking a law, an individual puts himself or herself outside the law and in conflict with the rules of society. The state takes over as the aggrieved party and charges the alleged culprit with an offence; and the justice system proceeds to trial, verdict and. where applicable, penalty.

FORMAL OR RESTORATIVE MEASURES?

The process of criminal justice focuses on the accused or offender, the person alleged to be—or who is—guilty as charged and, if guilty, who has to pay the penalty for the crime. In this process, except as witnesses giving testimony to the court, the victims of the crime, whether an individual, a group or people in the wider community, have little part to play. The development of Restorative Justice programmes is an attempt to refocus crime as a conflict among people, to bring together those directly affected and through third party mediation to address the impact of an offence on the victim, the offender and the community.

In this chapter, the context of Restorative Justice is described with reference to theories of punishment and the theoretical basis for mediation and reparation. The development of victim-offender mediation and other Restorative Justice models in the United Kingdom in the 1980s and 1990s is outlined, with reference to relevant literature. Findings from the questionnaires (*Chapter 3*) demonstrate the scope of victim-offender mediation, allowing profiles of current projects to be given so as to illustrate how these work in practice.

THE CONTEXT OF RESTORATIVE JUSTICE

There are two main schools of justification for punishment for breaking the law—retributivist and restorative.

Retribution
The retributivist demands revenge; the severity of the penalty should match the seriousness of the crime. Perceptions of appropriate penalties for crimes vary from time to time and from society to society and are fixed by the state. The ultimate revenge is to take the life of the offender and the moral and pragmatic debate about capital punishment continues.[1] As well as satisfying the desire for revenge, retribution is justified by its advocates as a deterrent.

Restorative Justice
The theory of restorative justice has developed from utilitarianism which seeks 'the greatest happiness of the greatest number'. To the utilitarian, the only justification for punishment is deterrence.[2] Suffering should not be inflicted on an offender just because he or she has committed a crime—but mainly to prevent greater suffering. Emphasis is therefore more on reforming the criminal so that he or she will not reoffend. The theory of Restorative Justice goes further than looking to change the behaviour of the offender; it seeks to move forward in a collaborative way to repair the damage to all parties involved in the offence, which includes supporting and making reparation to the victim, resolving conflict between the victim and the offender, resolving conflicts involving families or communities affected by the offence and giving the offender the opportunity to express remorse and make amends for his or her action.

---

[1] See Block B. P. and Hostettler, J., *Hanging in the Balance* and Hodgkinson P. and Rutherford A., *Capital Punishment Global Issues and Prospects*

[2] Though not, necessarily, for advocates of Restorative Justice: see, particularly, Wright, M., *Justice for Victims and Offenders: A Restorative Response to Crime*

Victims

To advocates of victims' rights, neither philosophy of punishment seems to focus sufficiently on the interests of the victim; nor does either work effectively to address the increase in the incidence of serious crime.

In the 1970s in North America, pioneer Victim Offender Reparation Programmes were established to promote the interests and welfare of victims of crime and also to develop alternative strategies for bringing about changes in patterns of offending. The principles of restorative justice, based largely on the work of Howard Zehr and Mark Umbreit, are now being adopted by and integrated into 15 state justice systems in the United States. Projects in, for example, Germany, France, Finland, Belgium and New Zealand are bringing restorative justice in from the margins towards mainstream policy in these countries. Learning from the American models, the voluntary organization Victim Support has emerged in the United Kingdom as the advocate for victims' rights and for greater awareness of the needs of victims of crime. The Forum for Initiatives in Reparation and Mediation (FIRM), now Mediation UK, worked closely with Victim Support on research into and development of reparation and mediation schemes. By 1997, 43 Restorative Justice projects had been established in the UK. The present Home Secretary, Jack Straw, has publicly endorsed the restorative approach on a number of occasions.

Models of Restorative Justice

Different models of restorative justice are being developed, piloted and researched and projects vary in the detail of their aims and methods. Some focus on young offenders and are termed 'diversion projects', which aim to intervene early in a case in order to divert young people—who admit to a first, minor offence—away from the full rigour of the conventional criminal justice process. Other models work with all age groups and assist mediation between victim and offender alongside court procedures. In addition to victim-offender mediation, a range of descriptions (or 'labels') is used for such initiatives. In America, victim-offender 'dialogues' or 'meetings' are becoming the preferred terms. Family Group Conferences (FGCs: already mentioned in *Chapter 4*) has developed from Maori tradition of including a wider range of stakeholders than just the victim and offender. FGCs may be called 'healing circles', the term from the cultural tradition of First Nation Canadians. 'Reintegrative shaming' is grounded in Japanese culture as a way of healing relationships after an offence has been committed; and in *Crime, Shame and Reintegration* (1989), John Braithwaite has looked at how this process can be positively integrated into western culture.

Whatever the label or model, victim-offender mediators believe that responses to crime should be *restorative* rather than *retributive*. They seek to address the needs of victims *and* offenders and to empower *both* parties to work out their conflict and to take a positive part in the process of justice. The mediation process, which has to be entered into voluntarily by both parties, is the essential part of a victim-offender programme which gives opportunity for the expression and sharing of feelings and for the healing of hurt on both sides. In the interests of victims, mediators are looking to achieve restitution, reparation and a greater measure of control by victims over the conduct and outcome of 'their' case. In pursuit of rehabilitation, they encourage offenders to take responsibility for their actions, to divert those who have committed minor offences from prosecution, and to reduce reoffending rates.

Strengths and weaknesses
The strengths of victim-offender mediation include flexibility, relevance and an enhanced sense of participation by the disputants; and for the victim greater satisfaction and a perception of fair dealing. However, it is usually used only in a narrow range of relatively minor offences and its relationship to the traditional criminal justice process is still uncertain in the UK. By detractors, it is argued that offenders may take part to avoid prosecution or to lighten their sentence rather than from a sincere wish to demonstrate remorse.

GROWTH OF VICTIM-OFFENDER SCHEMES

The first use of victim-offender mediation in the UK was in a diversion scheme set up by a Youth Support team in Exeter in 1979. An inter-agency team of police, youth and social workers aimed to divert young people who had committed minor offences from prosecution by a scheme of 'caution plus'[3]—which included mediation in the form of a meeting between victim and offender and an apology from the offender. The first *court-based* scheme for offenders was a pilot project in South Yorkshire in 1983, followed by four schemes set up with Home Office funding, one a *diversion project* in Cumbria and the other *three court-based* schemes in Leeds, Wolverhampton and Coventry. Response to the schemes was mixed. The research shows that victim satisfaction rates were high and reoffending rates slightly lower, but the schemes were criticised by those wishing to bear down on perpetrators of crime as

---

[3] ie a caution ('warning') administered by the police instead of prosecuting, attached in the case of 'caution plus' to some other obligation or undertaking.

'soft' on offenders. Critics also questioned how far the participants, especially the offenders, entered into the process voluntarily.

Concern at the rising costs of criminal justice led the Home Office to discontinue its special funding for victim-offender mediation; if the projects were to continue, they would have to work within core funding. Despite financial constraints, three of the schemes survived and confirmation of the beneficial effects of mediation were sufficient to encourage a diversity of initiatives. More schemes, both voluntary and statutory, have continued to develop. A report written at the end of 1996 for the European Committee of Experts on Mediation in Penal Matters, with the assistance of Mediation UK, listed all known UK victim-offender projects. The list distinguished major projects which do a substantial amount of victim-offender work from those that include it as part of their activity and those that are in the planning stage and not yet in operation. The small number of major schemes indicates that victim-offender mediation remains a marginal priority to service managers, especially those with limited budgets.

| | Total | Voluntary | Statutory: led by | | | |
			Police	Youth Justice	Social Services	Probation
Major Projects	9	4	1	1	1	4
Others	20	9	5	1	3	3
Planned	14	6	4	2	2	2

Note: In addition, two projects in 'Others' are led by Community Safety and by a Prison. Some of the 43 projects have multi-agency input and therefore appear under more than one heading.

Table 6.1: Major Victim-Offender Schemes, 1996

The report distinguishes two models of victim-offender mediation in current practice, the social work model and the independent mediation model, ie those where it is:

- used as part of a programme of work with offenders, confronting them with their behaviour and its effects in an attempt to reform them (the social work model)
- a service in its own right, offering victim and offender equally the chance to resolve any issues arising out of the offence (independent mediation model).

The report describes the differences between the two models:

> The social work model preserves control for the professionals, who design suitable interventions according to their own judgment, and who tend to use a directive or manipulative style of 'mediation' which is subjugated to the overall ends of the intervention programme. The independent model hands control over the content of meetings to the parties, the mediator assuming an impartial facilitator role . . .
>
> The feeling for the parties is very different. In the social work model they are passive recipients of professional guidance, which they may value or they may reject. In the independent model they are given opportunities for shaping their own lives and influencing events, which again some people are ready for and some are not, although careful preparation for meetings can maximise the abilities of parties to take advantage of the opportunities on offer . . .
>
> For those parties who tend to reject, or at least be suspicious of, authority and the pretensions of professionals, independent mediation may present a more genuine and useful experience.

The report also points out that the existence of the two models, and the freedom that both voluntary organizations and statutory agencies enjoy to develop a diversity of innovative projects, is an outcome of the 'benign neglect' of government policy which has neither opposed the development of victim-offender mediation nor encouraged and supported it with a legislative framework and adequate funding. The independent mediation model lends itself better to the ethos of community mediation services though many programmes operated by probation services are more sympathetic to this way of working than projects operated predominantly by social workers.

ISSUES FOR FURTHER EXPLORATION

A growing body of research tends to support the value of victim-offender mediation and raises issues for further exploration and discussion. Mediation UK has made a major contribution in the field by publicising research, networking and leading the discussion about the method's impact and effectiveness. For example, Annie Roberts and Mark Umbreit have summarised the findings of their recent research into eight victim-offender programmes in North America and two in the UK.[4] *Satisfaction* and a *perception of fairness* were expressed by both victims and offenders, and victims who participated had less fear of being victims again. The research showed that the programmes in

---

[4] *Mediation,* August 1996

America and Canada predominantly used *direct,* face-to-face mediation between victim and offender while in the UK projects the majority of mediation was *indirect,* the mediators acting as go-betweens. Those who had participated in direct mediation expressed higher levels of satisfaction at the benefits and outcomes than those who experienced indirect mediation. This leads the researchers to urge the UK projects to give 'strong consideration . . . to providing more opportunities and encouragement for victims and offenders to participate in direct, face-to-face mediation.' The American experience, however, may not be appropriate to victim-offender mediation as it has developed in the UK. American projects are observed to work predominantly with middle class clients who are interested in using mediation as a way of securing financial compensation for injury. In the experience of the co-ordinator of a UK project in the West Midlands, face-to-face confrontation between victim and offender is not what victims are seeking. They want the offender to know how they feel and they need assurance that they will not be 'revictimised'. She feels strongly that mediators should respond to the needs of victims rather than follow a theoretical model which may not fit the context. The same co-ordinator also feels that further research evidence is needed to establish more securely that victim-offender mediation reduces re-offending rates. The cost-effectiveness of mediating serious offences is likely to be greater than for minor offences but again research in this area is incomplete.

SOME FINDINGS

Most of the major organizations in the report mentioned above (see *Table 6.1*) and some of the smaller ones responded to the questionnaire used for the purposes of this book (*Chapter 3*). In addition, other respondents not listed in that report indicated that they include victim-offender mediation in their activities. The questionnaire responses confirmed the diversity of agencies and organizations involved in this work. Twenty-six respondents gave victim-offender mediation either as their only field of activity, or as one of its fields: see *Table 6.2*.

Police forces were the largest group in the statutory sector indicating this activity. They perceive part of their work as resolving conflict between victims of crime and perpetrators, though they are more likely to work as part of inter-agency groups or to refer cases to other specialist agencies than to run their own projects. Social services, too, are often part of interagency management teams. Probation services have led in victim-offender mediation since its inception, but the amount of this kind of work which any probation area can achieve depends on availability of funding. A south-western community mediation service used to get victim-offender referrals from a local probation service which has recently withdrawn from the partnership through lack of funding for the purpose. A service in the north-west does 'some' victim-offender mediation work. In Yorkshire and in Coventry where projects started in the 1980s, victim-offender mediation is a mainstream activity in probation work or continues with strong probation service support.

VOLUNTARY: 10	
Specialist victim-offender mediation projects	2
Community mediation services	5
Youth justice	1
Research, advocacy	2
STATUTORY: 13	
Probation	3
Social Services	3
Police	6
Youth Justice	2
PRIVATE: 3	
Training	2
Theatre (see pp. 75, 152-3)	1

Table 6.2: Types of Respondents Involved in Victim-Offender Mediation

Young people
A number of the schemes focus on work with young people. Three of the projects led by a probation service specialise in working with young offenders. A youth justice scheme in the South Midlands is in its formative stage, developing as a multi-agency project with strong input from the local police. A similar project in Wales, working with young people in a court setting, has both statutory and voluntary input. One of the private organizations which responded to the questionnaire offers group work in youth justice and conflict resolution leading to victim-offender mediation.

Two specialist voluntary sector projects responded with detailed information summarised in the next section. Five out of 60 responding community mediation services identified victim-offender mediation as one of their activities and one of these is also described in more detail.

Victim Support groups, which gave early impetus to victim-offender mediation work, were among respondents who indicated that their work does *not* include dispute resolution. Victim Support, both nationally and through local branches, campaigns for the rights of victims of crime, offering them practical, free and confidential support and advice. It is evident that at present the Victim Support movement does not generally feel confident that in victim-offender mediation processes the victim's needs are fully enough met.

THE SOCIAL WORK MODEL: EXAMPLES

A number of victim-offender mediation services are based on the social work model, for example those described in this section.

West Yorkshire
The West Yorkshire probation service has succeeded in continuing and expanding its victim-offender mediation project county-wide out of its core budget . It has been able partly to compensate for the loss of special funding by marketing its expertise to other victim-offender schemes as it is recognised nationally and abroad as a leading agency in the field of victim-offender mediation and reparation. Its beliefs and aims are set out in a recent annual report:

> Victims and offenders should have the opportunity to deal with their conflict themselves following an offence, within the wider context of the criminal justice system.
>
> Offenders have a moral responsibility to put right, as far as possible, the effects of their offence.
>
> Victim-offender mediation should be considered following any offence, the selection criteria being the willingness of the parties to participate and their safety.
>
> Victims have a right to be involved in the process of criminal justice.

The aims of our work with victims and offenders are:

1. To provide a service for voluntary mediation and/or reparation for victims and offenders.
2. To promote attitude changes in offenders with a view to changing their behaviour.
3. To influence the criminal justice system towards being more restorative.
4. To involve the victim in the process of justice.

Referrals are accepted from individual victims and offenders and from any agency involved in the criminal justice process at any stage in the that process (providing that the offence has been subject to the criminal process and guilt has been acknowledged). In 1995/6, the service received 325 referrals of which 114 (35 per cent) had completed the mediation process within the period. Ninety-two per cent of these were achieved by indirect mediation and just eight per cent involved direct, face-to-face mediation, a proportion that was commented on in the research mentioned on p. 65. In a typical case of theft from a shop accompanied by minor assault, the victim asked indirectly through the mediator for an apology and a donation to a charity. In one of the rare face-to-face meetings, the victim was able to tell the offender how frightened and threatened he had felt when the offender, when drunk, had thrown an object through the windscreen of his car. The offender explained what had occurred to make him drunk and disturbed and apologised for his behaviour. He also told the victim that he was attending a drink/drive group as a condition of his probation order.

> Post mediation both parties had clearly benefited from the meeting. The victim was able to get things off his chest and move on with his life. The offender felt good that he had been able to apologise and offer reassurance.

Northamptonshire

The Diversion Unit in Northamptonshire pioneered a multi-agency approach to increasing diversion with the twin purposes of offence resolution and the reduction of reoffending. Caseworkers from social services, education, the youth service, the probation service and the health service constitute the team which receives referrals of cases from the police. A member of the team interviews the offender and the injured party and prepares an action plan which is individually tailored to meet the needs and wishes of each victim and offender. The action plan, with an informal recommendation, is sent back to the police who almost always accept the unit's proposals. Most action plans involve some form of mediation. A briefing paper prepared in October 1996 states:

> Apology by way of letters or face to face meetings are used regularly whenever appropriate to assist in resolving offences. At other times resolution for the victim is achieved without any direct contact from the offender, but in the knowledge that Action to confront the offender with the consequences of their actions, and/or assist them to stop offending is undertaken by Diversion Unit staff.

Whatever action is planned, the unit keeps the injured party informed and involved, especially about what is being done to prevent a re-offence. The unit is concerned with the victim's feelings as well as with the offender's change of behaviour. A client survey in 1994/5 showed that 76 per cent of victims were either satisfied or very satisfied with their experience of working with the unit; 92 per cent of offenders were either satisfied or very satisfied. On its work with victims, the unit reported that:

> Much is said about the need to provide better involvement and services for victims. The Diversion Unit is a rare example of a part of the justice system which delivers on this concern.

Both these projects offer victim-offender mediation as part of programmes of work with offenders and as such match the social work model. However, both show deep concern for the needs of injured parties and although victims have to participate in mediation on the terms of the programme, their feelings and wishes are given full weight in decisions about the conduct of cases.

Scotland

A mediation and reparation project set up in Scotland in 1988 by SACRO was unique in Britain at that time in being 'a pre-trial diversion scheme applying to adults'. The aims of the project are:

1. To provide a dispute resolution service through mediated reparative agreements between victim and accused as a strategy for diversion from prosecution.
2. To focus the service on areas of particular social deprivation in order to reflect their relatively high levels of crime and criminality.
3. To increase the scope of partnership arrangements between the Regional Council and other public, private and voluntary sector agencies in the provision of services to the Criminal Justice System.
4. To monitor and evaluate the quality and nature of the service over the lifetime of the Project.

The objectives include the development of reparation as an alternative to prosecution and mediation as a technique of dispute resolution within the criminal justice system. The Procurator-Fiscal refers cases for mediation to the service rather than proceeding with prosecution. Each case must involve no more than one or two people facing charges and must not be too serious to be suitable for mediation. The victim is contacted first by both the Procurator-Fiscal's office and the mediation service to find out if they are willing to participate in mediation. If they are not, then the process ends and the case goes to court. If the victim agrees, then the willingness of the offender is ascertained, and only if both parties are willing does the mediation process get under way, and this may take the form of indirect mediation with the mediator acting as go-between or direct face-to-face mediation with the mediator present as facilitator. A successful mediation may end in an apology from the offender plus payment of some form of reparation, often financial but frequently in the form of 'useful work' with the elderly or disabled or in an environmental project.

Up to the time of the 1996 annual report, 733 cases had been referred to the service in four and a half years. In about 64 per cent of cases, the victim agreed to mediation and 90 per cent of the accused in these cases were willing to proceed. In nearly 80 per cent of cases in which victims agreed to mediation, agreements were reached and in most of these the terms of the agreement were fully complied with. Success depends on the close co-operation between the project and a large number of statutory and voluntary agencies in the area. The courts, police and local social services are all fully supportive as are voluntary agencies which may be involved in part of the reparation process. The project has monitored a high satisfaction rate by victims who feel that they have obtained practical amends and that the cause of natural justice has been well served. The project report concludes:

> The findings to date through the scheme have shown that the accused are able to respond to the challenge of being held accountable directly for their offence and to make good the wrong done in an appropriate way, and it has shown that mediation as a technique for conflict resolution and the creation of reparative agreements is applicable in the criminal justice system.

This project is run by a voluntary organization, independent but in close co-operation with criminal justice agencies. A sister project also run by SACRO:

> works with young people aged between 11 and 16 years of age who have been charged by the police and referred to the children's reporter. It works alongside the existing services for young offenders provided by the Children's Reporter Service and Social Work Department, and is supported by the police. The project is funded by the Council's Social Work Department.
> The project also provides the opportunity for victims of crime to be informed and about how cases are resolved. There is also the possibility of obtaining some form of amends.
> The aim of the project is to achieve a mediated agreement or settlement between the offender and victim which helps to make amends for the offence which has been committed.

Although both projects fall within the independent model, in their emphasis on the rehabilitation of the offender they have more in common with the social work model.

FAMILY GROUP CONFERENCE MODEL

An example of a pilot project using the Family Group Conference (FGC) model comes from Hampshire. It is a development of the use of FGCs in family welfare cases described in *Chapter 4* (see p. 40). In this project also a voluntary organization, the Hampton Trust, has taken the lead in co-ordinating a multi-agency partnership, including the local probation service, social services, the police and health services, with interests from education, the youth service and the business community, to work with young offenders. Using the New Zealand model of FGCs, the project works with young people from the age of ten to 17 who have already been cautioned for one burglary or 'taking a conveyance without consent' and who have committed a similar offence within six months of the first. After a meeting of all parties—including the victim, the victim's supporters and members of the wider community—with an independent co-ordinator in the role of mediator, the offender's family are left alone to make a reparation plan for the offender. As the FGC has no formal recognition in law and operates outside the justice system, the offender will also receive a further caution.

The independent role of the co-ordinator is seen by the planning group as crucial to the success of the process. All the parties should be able to engage fully and freely with the co-ordinator who will need to prepare the victim and victim's supporters for their part in the process. The co-ordinator may need to encourage and persuade the victim to be present at the conference and to ensure that the offender's supporters do not outnumber and intimidate, and thereby revictimise, the victim. The co-ordinator also has a significant role in choosing a suitable venue for the conference, in liaising with professionals who may be involved in the reparation plan, and in writing up the plan in clear terms satisfactory to all parties.

From its implementation in April 1997, the project is being independently monitored and evaluated by the University of Portsmouth to assess its effect on crime prevention and reduction, the satisfaction of all parties involved, and the cost of FGCs compared with traditional judicial processes. In discussion at a workshop where the project was described, concerns were expressed that it was too offender-driven on the social work model, and consequently the feelings and needs of the victim were not being sufficiently addressed. Reservations were voiced especially by members of Victim Support groups about the pressure that might be put on the victim, in terms of encouragement and persuasion, to take part in the process.

INDEPENDENT MODEL: EXAMPLES

Some examples of programmes conforming to an independent mediation model were represented in the research responses.

The North

A victim-offender mediation project in a northern city was set up in October 1995 as a voluntary organization on the initiative of the local probation service and with funding from the local Police Community Initiatives Programme. It is an independent agency working alongside statutory agencies from which it will receive referrals. The project emphasises that its mediators 'are not social workers, judges or jurors, probation officers, counsellors, pushy, paid, biased, discriminating, prejudiced' but 'volunteers, specially trained, empathisers, enablers, ordinary people, listeners, providers of an effective and efficient service, vehicles for a voice, accessible'. The first task of the two part-time co-ordinators was to recruit and train volunteers as victim-offender mediators. Both indirect and direct mediation are offered to victims and offenders who are willing to participate. The project by the time of its first annual report had four cases in progress. Its work will be monitored and evaluated by the Centre for Criminology and Legal Research at a local university.

West Midlands

A West Midlands community mediation service set up in the mid-1980s soon extended its work from neighbourhood to victim-offender mediation. The co-ordinator, herself a local magistrate, was aware how quickly a neighbourhood dispute can escalate into actions which bring the disputants into the criminal justice process. Recognising the criticism that mediation can be seen as a 'soft option' for offenders, she also observed that it was a positive process for victims. While professionally-led schemes defined diversion of the offender from custody as a priority, an independent community mediation service would be free of the pressure of service objectives and could focus more specifically on the victim's perspective.

Uniquely this West Midlands mediation service formed a close working relationship with the local Victim Support group, pooling resources and sharing accommodation. A probation officer was seconded to assist in its development and a multi-disciplinary working party with representation from local courts agreed criteria for victim-offender mediation. Referrals can be made from any agency or individual involved in a case in which the victim can be personally identified. Mediation can begin at any stage providing the offender makes a guilty plea and both sides agree to participate. There are special criteria for sexual and racial offences and up to the present domestic violence cases are excluded.

The majority of referrals come in the first place from offenders, often referred through the police, probation service, direct from the courts or through a programme developed in partnership with a local young offender institution. The co-ordinator feels ambivalent about publicising the possibility of mediation to victims. As few perpetrators of crime are caught, publicity could raise expectations which could not be fulfilled; on the other hand, victims have the right to know that the service exists and should not be over-protected.

Once an offender has expressed an interest in mediation, mediators and victim support volunteers work closely together first to check whether the victim would be likely to benefit from mediation; for example if the victim is particularly frail or vulnerable physically or mentally, the offender would be told immediately that mediation could not proceed. The victim is contacted by the victim support worker who is present if needed as a support through the whole mediation process.

Of 200 referrals per year, about 40 proceed to mediation and more than 90 per cent of these are resolved by indirect mediation, the rest through face-to-face meetings. The results of a small scale research project in 1994 showed that 'relatively simple interventions with victims can help reduce the effects of victimisation.' A case study of mediation following a house burglary illustrates the work of the mediator and the needs and feelings of the victim.

It was two months since her home was broken into when the mediator went to visit Mrs X. Mr and Mrs X had received no information from the police so they welcomed the opportunity to receive information. Mrs X explained that since the burglary her husband had been sleeping downstairs on the settee armed with a baseball bat, waiting.

Mrs X was so relieved to hear that the person responsible was on remand in custody. 'My husband can come back to bed now; it has been two months that we've been apart at night.'

There were many questions she wanted to ask of the offender. Most of these questions were answered immediately as the mediator had received permission from the offender to disclose details about him. Mrs X wanted the offender to know how the burglary had affected the family, how frightened they had all been. She wanted to know why he chose their house. What would he have done if one of them had come downstairs? Why did he do it? Mrs X's main concern was the loss of her handbag which contained irreplaceable family photographs of her father who had died six

74

months before. She asked the mediator to enquire about these when he next met the offender.

On the second interview with the offender in the remand centre, the mediator exchanged the information from Mrs X. The offender drew a map for the mediator showing where he had discarded the handbag. He was extremely disturbed to hear about the effects of his crime on Mr and Mrs X and happy to answer all the questions put to him.

The mediator immediately returned to Mrs X with the information. The handbag was found and though in poor condition, the photographs were still there. Mrs X sat on the floor with her handbag. She explained the importance of every item she took out. She pulled out the photo album and tears rolled down her face. 'Please thank him, thank him for returning Dad's photo.'

Arts project

A final brief profile describes a private, non-profit making organization which uses theatre to look at the relationship between victims, offenders and observers of crime. A three stage cycle of events over a period of nine months involves victims and offenders in a variety of interactive creative activities to encourage them to express their feelings and tell their stories. Through videos and puppet shows made by the participants, the causes, consequences, seriousness and remedies of crimes are re-enacted and discussed, and a multi-media exhibition of the work aims to:

Investigate the relationship between victims, offenders and observers of crime. To interpret the material gathered during the field-work and communicate it to audiences through the medium of photography and video installation as well as in a series of live performances.

The project feels that the approach succeeds in drawing all participants into experiences which enhance their understanding of their own behaviour and the behaviour of others. It demonstrates the contribution that arts projects can make, especially among young people, to the development of conflict prevention strategies in the field of restorative justice work.

CONCLUSION

In this chapter, the context, aims and processes of restorative justice and victim-offender mediation have been examined. Restorative justice is defined as 'a process whereby all the parties with a stake in a particular offence come together to resolve collectively how to deal with the aftermath of the offence and its implications for the future.' Mediation and other forms of intervention in this field are in a developmental stage and the progress of projects involved in pioneering different models is the subject of evaluative research. Victim-offender mediation, even when practised by voluntary agencies on the independent mediation model, is necessarily located within the framework of the criminal justice process.

Mediation has to be voluntary, but the circumstances surrounding the process suggest that participants may be subject to pressure to take part. Outcomes have to satisfy the needs of victims of crime both in terms of resolution of their emotional trauma and satisfaction that justice has been done. Advocates of victims' rights argue that victims need support and assistance beyond participation in a process in which they are only of equal significance with the person who has caused their problem. Outcomes also need to demonstrate reform and rehabilitation of offenders as well as the performance of reparation for the offence. To receive general acceptance, mediation cannot be perceived as a 'soft option' which lets the offender escape a realistic punishment for the crime.

The report on *The Evolution of Restorative Justice* already mentioned identifies other current issues in the relationship between victim-offender mediation and the traditional criminal justice system. Should the outcome of mediation influence criminal justice decisions and if so does this prejudice the voluntariness of the process? Should some offences such as rape, racial harassment and child abuse be excluded from victim-offender mediation because the power imbalance of the parties prevents fair negotiation? Primarily in the social work model, is there a danger that professional agencies will use victim-offender mediation processes to meet their own agendas? Will research into the outcomes of victim-offender mediation in terms of the satisfaction of participants and its impact on crime convince victims' organizations and public authorities, including the justice system and the government of the day, to support the development of a fully funded nation-wide service?

Concerns about the manner in which restorative justice is implemented have been expressed by Mark Umbreit. From his long experience of working to gain wider acceptance of the principles of Restorative Justice, he is now apprehensive that in moving into the mainstream it is losing its vision. There is too little empirical evidence to support Restorative Justice policies and practices. It is being grasped by professionals to serve their own agendas for dealing especially with juvenile offenders and the interests of the victim and victim-sensitive procedures are being subordinated to the drive for solutions to youth crime. Umbreit warns that:

... interventions that appear to be intrinsically restorative may, in fact, not be. Unless any intervention is clearly grounded in restorative justice values and procedures developed to maximise the implementation of those values, it is predictable that many so-called restorative interventions could easily become coopted to meet primarily justice system bureaucratic needs, rather than those most affected by crime: the victim, victimized community, and offender. This could easily lead to the 'fast food version' of restorative justice practice that would : provide a 'quick-fix'; remain offender focused; use victims as 'props' rather than active partners; have little patience to listen to victim's stories, validate their needs, or invite their participation in the process.

SOURCES AND FURTHER READING: *Chapter 6*

Braithwaite, J., *Crime, Shame and Reintegration*, 1989

Davies, G., *Making Amends: Mediation and Reparation in Criminal Justice*, 1992

Engle Merry, S., and Milner, N. (Eds.), *The Possibility of Popular Justice: A Case Study of Community Mediation in the United States*, 1993

Institute for the Study and Treatment of Deliquency (ISTD: King's College, London), Conference: 'Repairing the Damage: Restorative Justice in Action', 20 March 1997

Marshall, T., 'The Evolution of Restorative Justice in Britain'. Paper prepared for European Committee of Experts on Mediation in Penal Matters, November 1996

Northamptonshire Diversion Unit, *Annual Report and Briefing Paper, 1996*

Raynor, P., *Probation as an Alternative to Custody*, 1988

Roberts A., and Umbreit, M., 'Victim-offender Mediation: The English Experience', *Mediation*, Summer 1996, Vol. 12:3

Umbreit, M., *Mediating Interpersonal Conflicts: A Pathway to Peace*, 1995

Umbreit, M., *Victim Meets Offender: The Impact of Restorative Justice and Mediation*, 1994

West Yorkshire Probation Service Victim-Offender Unit, *Annual Report 1995/6*

Wright, M., *Justice for Victims and Offenders: A Restorative Response to Crime*, 1996

Zehr, H., *Changing Lenses*, 1990.

Acknowledgments

Tony Marshall, Home Office Research and Planning Unit

Mark Umbreit and all the participants in the conference on Restorative Justice at Bristol, March 1997

Northamptonshire Diversion Unit

SACRO Grampian Mediation and Reparation Project

SACRO Fife Young Offenders Mediation Project

Sandwell Mediation Service

Plymouth Mediation Service

Maidstone Mediation Service
Greater Manchester Probation Service
West Yorkshire Probation Service
Milton Keynes Youth Crime Reduction
Sheffield Victim-Offender Mediation
Neath Port Talbot Youth Justice Service
Impossible Theatre
The Bridge Consultancy
The Hampton Trust
Hampshire Social Services.

CHAPTER 7

Mediation in Schools

In P7 we have trained to mediate.
It helps sort out conflicts and agreement it creates.
We all obey the ground rules which we drew up at the start
We've trained to mediate.
Glory, glory mediation, Glory glory mediation
Glory, glory mediation, To sort out all the fights, yipee!

Class P7, Ballysally Primary School

The development of peer mediation in schools is one of the most exciting fields of expansion in alternative dispute resolution. In schools, the mediators are children, mediating the disputes of other children. They approach the issues with a refreshing directness and clarity and practise the skills with a seriousness and commitment which demonstrate at the same time the simplicity and the sophistication of the process. Once trained in the procedures and given space to practise them, they are enthusiastic and confident that mediation is a better way to manage relationships.

This chapter first analyses the questionnaire responses in this field and, after discussing the development of mediation in schools and peer mediation projects in Northern Ireland, London and Devon, examines the future of mediation in schools. The concluding section looks beyond the school, to young people in the community.

Sixteen respondents to the questionnaire (*Chapter 3*) indicated 'schools mediation' or 'peer mediation' under 'other ADR, please specify'. These responses can be categorised as in *Table 7.1* below.

Voluntary organizations	Specialised	1
	General	7
	Training	3
	Religious/training	1
	Arts	1
Education	Universities	2
	School	1

Table 7.1: Respondents Involved in Mediation Work in Schools

Each of the 15 non-school based projects worked with a number of schools, some on long-term projects but more often for limited periods of engagement. Mediation UK has established conflict resolution in schools as one of its three major strands of development and the respondents include most of the major organizations listed in the Mediation UK Directory as involved in school work. Six of them were community neighbourhood mediation projects, three of which work significantly with local school-based projects while three expressed the intention of developing school work in the future. Three community mediation projects which indicate in the Directory that they offer schools mediation did not do so in the questionnaire, though one wrote that they were hoping to develop work in this area soon. Community mediation services are aware of the potential for mediation in schools and would wish to give it priority when resources and opportunity permit. Discussion of the major school projects below illustrates the sensitivity of the work and explains why, up to now, it has been most successfully developed by specialist agencies.

EARLY DEVELOPMENTS

The introduction of peer mediation in schools was pioneered in California and American models of training and implementation are one inspiration for practice in the UK. Work with British schools has been developed from the initiatives of two or three seminal organizations working in close relationship with each other. Much of the inspiration for peace education has come from the Society of Friends, through the Education Advisory Programme of Quaker Peace and Service, the international department of the Society in Britain.

The Education Advisory Programme (EAP) works on all aspects of peace education, which it sees as being both *for* peace and *about* peace. Education *about* peace include challenging assumptions, exploring the topics of war, arms and disarmament, conscientious objection, human rights, citizenship, and social justice. Education *for* peace includes teaching the skills of peace by examining conflict resolution, mediation and problem solving. The EAP highlights the way in which the many aspects of peace education are fundamentally connected.

The Kingston Friends Workshop Group initiated the first conflict resolution project for schools in the United Kingdom in 1981, and the group produced a training manual which is widely used in a range of training programmes for young people and schools. The Quaker approach was welcomed in Northern Ireland where the political situation put the need for peace education high on the political agenda. *De facto*, most of education in Northern Ireland is segregated. Schools are either state controlled and protestant or maintained and catholic. A small number of integrated schools have been set up since 1981 in an attempt to break the sectarian stranglehold on education, but to date only 2.3 per cent of the children of Northern Ireland attend integrated schools. The sectarian divide in education is both a reflection and a cause of the continuing conflict in the province. In a much quoted dictum of a prominent educationist, Malcolm Skilbeck, Northern Ireland's teachers are the 'naive bearers of (sectarian) culture'. In an attempt to bring schools and therefore communities into closer understanding of each other, in 1989 the Department of Education in Northern Ireland introduced the cross-curriculum themes of Education for Mutual Understanding and Cultural Heritage, to be supported by a programme of Cross Community Contact. From 1992, the themes became a statutory requirement though Cross Community Contact remains optional. The objectives of EMU and Cultural Heritage are to enable pupils:

> To learn to respect and value themselves and others; to appreciate the inter-dependence of people within society; to know about and understand what is shared as well as what is different about their cultural traditions; and to appreciate how conflict may be handled in non-violent ways.

> Northern Ireland Curriculum Council, 1990

Peace education fitted the new curriculum aims and became a significant part of EMU. From 1988 to 1994, the Quaker Peace Education Project ran an action research programme of workshops based on the principles of Affirmation, Communication and Co-operation with teachers and adult groups, and for young people both in schools and in the community. Links with similar projects and groups in other European countries resulted in the establishment of a European Network for Conflict Resolution in Education (ENCORE). In 1992, QPEP hosted ENCORE's first summer school at the Magee campus of the University of Ulster in Derry.

As part of its work within the primary school sector, QPEP began in 1993 a pilot peer mediation project in two primary schools in Derry. When QPEP ended in 1994, this action research project, together with other aspects of QPEP's work, was continued by the EMU Promoting School Project within the University of Ulster's Centre for the Study of Conflict based at Magee Campus in Derry. Detailed accounts and assessments of QPEP, EMU and the pilot stages of the Peer Mediation in Primary Schools project have been published in the books listed at the end of the chapter.

PEER MEDIATION OBSERVED

Peer mediation projects have been set up in six primary schools with five more coming on board in 1997. The following description of peer mediation in two primary schools is based on discussions with the children, the teachers, the principal of one of the schools, the trainers from the EMU Promoting School Project, and on witnessing the assembly at one of the schools at which the children gave a presentation to the whole school to mark the opening of their mediation service.

Oakgrove Integrated School in Derry is still in temporary accommodation but its permanent buildings are due to start 'soon'. It is situated in the Waterside, the mainly protestant area of Derry, but draws children from both communities from a wide catchment area. Its ethos is non-sectarian and child-centred and seeks to integrate the best of both traditions in Northern Ireland. Ballysally Primary School is state controlled, set in the centre of a run-down loyalist housing estate on the outskirts of Coleraine. Life on the estate is impoverished, tough and often violent, and the school principal, who has been 18 years in post, is committed to making the school an oasis of colour, light and freedom of spirit. He and his staff succeed in creating a rich and stress-free learning environment for the children.

In both schools, the teachers of P7, the top class of 10 year olds, and the ancillary staff, including classroom and playground assistants, were committed to the introduction of peer mediation. In the first year, the trainers from EMU Promoting School Project trained both children and staff. In the second year, after facilitating initial workshops, the project could begin to meet its objective of making the schools self-sustaining by leaving the training programme in the hands of the school-based team.

The children have a guide to mediation, entitled *Conflict-Busters*, but the experiential training workshops give them their skills and understanding of the process. In discussion, they recalled in detail the contents of the workshops and the reasons for games and activities. They explained the importance of affirmation, of 'feeling good about yourself' and making other people feel good about themselves. They talked about the importance of good communication and about the games that demonstrated the benefits of co-operation. They were familiar with the ground rules and their purpose—no put-downs, keep secrets, it's all right to make mistakes, you can pass, volunteer only yourself, don't interrupt.

In the workshops the children practised the stages of mediation in role play situations that they devised themselves. The disputes they are familiar with involve the falling out of friends, exclusion from friendship groups, quarrels about space and equipment in the playground, name calling and bullying, sometimes physical contact leading to a fight. All the children said that they enjoyed role-playing.

After the whole class was trained to mediate, everyone had the opportunity to apply to be appointed a mediator. Applicants were interviewed by a panel of teachers and children with the teacher only using a veto in exceptional circumstances. Once the mediators were appointed, the team presented their service to the whole school assembly, describing their training and role-playing a complete mediation process.

In the demonstration, two mediators first checked that the disputants were willing to take part in mediation. They explained the process and rules to the parties:

- mediators don't take sides
- mediators don't tell you what to do
- mediators don't tell secrets
- no interrupting, no calling names, no blaming the other person.

Each party told their side of the story and one of the mediators repeated it back to check it was right. (The demonstration dispute involved the interruption of a game of hopscotch by a game of football, followed by a quarrel and name calling.) The parties were asked to say how they felt (hurt and angry) and what they thought the problem was (calling names, losing temper, hopscotch and football played in the same part of the playground). Then they brainstormed possible solutions, however unlikely (he should go to boarding school, she should only play hopscotch at home, he should apologise, she shouldn't lose her temper) from which, by a process of give-and-get, an agreement was negotiated. At each stage a writer listed what the parties said and at the end wrote out the agreement which the parties signed. The mediators said they would check in a couple of days to see if the agreement had been kept. The children clearly felt ownership of the process and took it deeply seriously. The whole school assembly down to the very smallest children watched and listened with rapt attention. The teacher explained that from Monday mediators wearing distinctive hats would be available to any child from P4 upwards who wanted a dispute mediated. At the end, one child read his own simple prayer for the success of the mediation service and the children sang their mediation song—special to Ballysally—with vast enthusiasm, and were presented with certificates.

In Oakgrove the children were clear about the advantages to them of their mediation service. Children have a better understanding of children's disputes than adults do. Children have time for each other; teachers and other adults are often too busy or distracted or having a bad day and shout at children, making them feel small. If disputes can be dealt with quickly, it prevents quarrels getting worse. Mediation is seen to be fair, and the children put great value on fairness. Mediation lets people be friends again and that is what the children wanted.

The children were realistic about possible difficulties. Bullying was difficult to deal with. They knew that some serious disputes must be taken to a teacher. They found it difficult to mediate fairly if one of the parties was a best friend; either they had to remember that mediators must be fair or ask another member of the team to take over. They had to spot children who made up disputes just for the fun of being mediated. But unanimously the children thought that mediation was good for the class and the school. The training workshops had made them all feel good about themselves and the class was a happier place. The mediation service had improved the atmosphere in the playground and some of them had used their skills in situations outside school—in street quarrels or in their families—and felt very good about this. They had received public recognition for their achievement; for example representatives from all the schools which had mediation schemes travelled to Dublin to demonstrate peer mediation to Mary Robinson, the Irish President.

As well as demonstrating their skills as mediators, the children were articulate, able to sustain discussion and demonstrate conceptual understanding, and were confident and relaxed. A mediation was taking place in another room during the class discussion and it was clear from the children's attitude that this was accepted by everyone as a normal and important part of the life of the school.

ISSUES ARISING FROM PEER MEDIATION

While circumstances may suggest that peer mediation is particularly appropriate in schools in Northern Ireland, it is clearly a process that appeals to children's sense of justice and fair play and would benefit all schools. It can, however, only flourish where it is supported by the whole school ethos. Peer mediation is about the development of relationship skills among children and about building self-esteem and esteem for others, but to be successful, relationships must be consistent throughout the school. Peer mediation can be the catalyst for raising issues about the whole school ethos and challenges adult relationships as much as relationships between children.

The schools visited and described demonstrate the success of the project; in other schools, although they welcomed the project, it has been more difficult to make it self-sustaining. A more authoritarian and hierarchical ethos within a school might make the idea of children being empowered to deal with their own disputes appear more threatening to adults and the involvement of ancillary staff less acceptable.

The EMU Promoting School Project is questioning the wisdom of working first with the children and not simultaneously or better still initially with the adults in the school community. It feels that to establish peer mediation in all schools in Northern Ireland (as they recommend) would require more preparatory training workshops for the whole adult communities of the schools so that programmes can be sustained from the beginning by whole school commitment.

A more immediate issue concerns the progression of the primary school children who have experienced mediation. The 11 plus selection process is universal in Northern Ireland though most children in integrated primary schools choose to go to integrated secondary schools. Wherever they went in the following September, the P7s would have found themselves at the bottom of the heap with no support for or acknowledgment of their skills. Some engagement with the 15 year olds in one secondary school has been too little, too late. Another concern is how to programme the training of the present primary school P6s in mediation so that there is a smooth transition to a new team of mediators at a time when teachers are putting all their effort into 11 plus preparation work. Perhaps especially relevant to Northern Ireland is the concern that while mediation will work in the safe and sheltered environment of the school, it might be less effective and even dangerous for the practitioner in the 'real world'. Issues of peacemaking *in the community* are explored in *Chapter 8.*

OTHER SCHOOL MEDIATION WORK

Peer mediation in schools in mainland Britain is developing slowly. The problem of bullying in schools is of concern to parents and schools alike and alternative conflict resolution strategies are perceived to offer possible solutions. A voluntary project in the north-west seeks to make its town a Bully-Free Zone by reducing bullying and the fear of bullying and increasing awareness of non-violent strategies for resolving conflict. A team of young volunteers, trained in mediation skills, publicise the service in schools and help other young people who are involved in bullying and conflict.

The National Coalition Building Institute (UK) (NCBI) offers its prejudice reduction training to schools as a positive step towards reducing the incidence of bullying. About 30 schools, both primary and secondary, have benefited from the training which gives young people the opportunity to deal with prejudice and stereotyping 'openly and in ways which are safe, unthreatening and respectful of people as individuals . . . And a valuable, and completely unexpected bonus has been increased mutual respect between staff and students', writes the NCBI director responsible for the training programme.

A Kent mediation service was asked to train pupils in mediation skills to add to peer counselling skills they were already learning. This enabled them to extend the service they were offering to help resolve interpersonal conflicts as well as personal problems. A London mediation service offers a programme to transform conflict in schools by a range of approaches for staff, governors, parents and playground supervisors as well as peer mediation training for children in recognition that 'it is vital that any initiative has whole school support'. The schools worker goes into schools in response to requests from a committed group of staff and the agreement of the headteacher. In some schools she trains a core group of teachers in conflict resolution skills and attitudes using participative trust-building and communication activities such as role plays and games on the model used by Cohen in American schools. These teachers then pass on the training to pupils and other adults in the school with the ongoing support of the mediation service. In other schools teachers and children are trained together, which in the co-ordinator's judgment is more effective.

The teachers have difficulty finding time to sustain a programme of peer mediation and the schools' work co-ordinator has tried to involve other educational services in supporting the work. Although EWOs, Educational Psychologists, community education and youth service workers have all expressed interest, they have not yet participated, perhaps because the local authority, although supportive in principle, has not to date adopted peer mediation programmes as part of their policy. So far, mediation programmes are established in two secondary and four primary schools in the area.

Highfield Junior School in Devon is unusual in its approach to involving children in the running of their school. Training children as peer mediators is part of a programme of consultation and power-sharing aimed at resolving and preventing conflict in the school. When a new headteacher came to the school in 1991, she found a situation of conflict and disorder that was completely disrupting the educational progress of children in the school. Her approach to turning the school round was to involve the children in decision-making about the rules and procedures by which their activity is controlled. Using the participatory strategy of circle-time (when all the children sit down with the teacher together) where issues and concerns could be freely discussed, the children themselves wrote the rules which they are then committed to observe. Good behaviour is positively acknowledged and rewarded and bad behaviour is challenged and punished. Circle-time evolved into the 'school council', at which two representatives from each class meet each week to sort out whole school problems such as bullying and to negotiate and make decisions about rules, freedoms and responsibilities. An example is described by one of the children:

> We said we wanted to eat our lunch outside. We had to agree the extra responsibilities with the meal time supervisors. Like no one will run across the tables. No one will eat standing up. We must clear up any litter. We must follow meal time supervisors' instructions. We can have lunch outside if we want to and I like that very much.
>
> If we break our responsibility agreement, our freedom stops. school's council decides how many days sanction we must have before we can eat outside again.

The children asked if they could be involved in choosing new staff, and after a check that there are no rules preventing this, children now have an advisory role in interviewing and selecting staff.

Parents and ancillary staff as well as teachers and children are involved in a whole school participatory process which has succeeded in establishing an ethos of openness, caring and sharing. The negotiated and democratic approach has transformed expectations and behaviour patterns:

> We firmly believe that setting this firm foundation of ownership, pride and self responsibility strengthens the children's will, capacity and tenacity to learn, to produce acceptable patterns of behaviour and to share practical group activities which lead to positive outcomes.

As well as the programme of transformation which can be identified as conflict prevention strategy, peer mediation has been introduced as a conflict resolution strategy within the whole school approach to behaviour management. First there were 'guardian angels', helpers chosen by children who were trying to change their behaviour or who had problems.

> Guardian angels are there to help you. They might be your friend or someone else. You can have two or three guardian angels. If you are being bullied they fly to rescue you and help you mediate your problem. If you are trying to improve your behaviour they are around to help you.

The headteacher explained how guardian angels developed into trained mediators:

Some of the house captains were chosen as guardian angels. They had been chosen by all the children in the school for their qualities of leadership and understanding and listening skills and for their concern about other people and their problems.

They were doing a grand job as guardian angels and they were developing ways of doing it . . . We realised that they needed training, so that everyone was doing the same thing. We had to adopt ways of resolving conflict fairly and peacefully, without giving ill-informed advice, and without making conflict worse. And the way forward was towards mediation.

At first, eight mediators were trained together with some members of staff, who then took over the training of more mediators as demands on the original group were so heavy. The steps in the classic mediation process are used by the trained mediators to resolve disputes fairly and confidentially.

Mediation is about listening, asking questions and getting people to think of new ways to sort out their own conflicts, and to decide what they are going to do.

It is not about giving advice, or taking sides, or blaming people, or forcing them to agree. Mediation means staying in the middle. It is about making like fair and being a good listener.

Teachers and children agree that mediation is an effective way of sorting out disputes and that because disputes are mediated by peers, fewer conflicts have to be dealt with by teachers. The school feels proud of the positive changes that have been achieved. It has been praised in a report by OFSTED inspectors and earned an *Investor in People* award. The headteacher receives enquiries about the scheme from schools all over the country which is an indication of its rarity.

It is worth asking why the project at Highfield Junior School is so unusual and why almost all conflict resolution projects in schools depend on engagement with voluntary or independent agencies and initiatives within individual schools rather than forming part of national educational policy. The answer may already have been suggested in the discussion of the project in Northern Ireland. Schools are essentially hierarchical institutions where disciplinary procedures are rigidly established and documented. The idea of empowering the pupils to participate in resolving conflict involves altering the focus of control. It may mean changing the school ethos, and all this means changes of attitude for staff, parents and pupils. In teacher-training establishments, students are taught how to maintain discipline rather than how to resolve conflict. Peer mediation has perhaps been perceived as being a symptom of weak discipline and until recently positive UK models have been lacking. It was good to observe that the publication of the account of the Devon project received coverage in a national newspaper. However it was noticeable that the report focused on the mechanisms for improving school discipline without mentioning the peer mediation scheme.

WORK WITH YOUNG PEOPLE

Conflict resolution work involving young people illustrates well how mediation crosses artificially constructed boundaries. Young people are members of families and local communities and—depending on age and individual circumstances—may be pupils at schools or colleges. They have already been seen in *Chapter 6* to be the focus of Restorative Justice projects. Innovative projects with young people combine many of the issues and concerns that have been discussed in *Chapters 4* to *7*. Few (only eight out of 205) respondents to the questionnaire indicated that they undertake conflict resolution work with young people *outside* the context of family, school, or youth justice. Three community mediation services mentioned young people as one of the groups to whom they offer services. Confronting conflict creatively is the theme of two training projects focusing on young people, one working through drama and the other through experiential workshops; five other training organizations work with youths and youth leaders together on how to handle conflict and aggression.

A unit attached to a NACRO project in London, staffed mainly by volunteers, works one-to-one with young people from ten years old who are experiencing problems in dealing with authority: 'We try to be "honest broker" between young people and local services', which might be schools, police, courts or social services. A youth worker or a volunteer mediator acts as a mediator between the young person and the agency with the consent of the young person on a confidential basis.

A community mediation service in the West Midlands described how it was called in by the local authority community safety officer to mediate between the residents of a whole street and a group of young people whose behaviour the residents found threatening. After interviewing all the residents to hear their stories about their fears of noise, vandalism and petty crime, the mediators tried to speak with the young people to hear their side, but at first the young people were not willing to participate. The mediation service liaised with detached youth workers who were able to make contact with the young people and gain their trust for the mediation process. After meetings with the young people to find out what they saw as the causes and solutions of the conflict, the mediators were able to bring the two sides together to share their feelings and needs. Both sides wanted the same thing—a local centre for the young people where they could enjoy themselves without disturbing the neighbourhood. Together, with the support of the local pub and brewery, the two sides have applied for funding to build a youth centre on a piece of waste ground near—but not too near—the street.

The success of this mediation between residents and young people was immediately felt. In one month before the meetings, the police had 600 calls from residents of the street and the housing department 120; in the month after the two sides started working together, there were only two calls to the police and none to housing. The case provides an excellent example of how mediation can bring together conflicting interests to work on a problem and transform a conflict situation into consensus and constructive collaboration. It illustrates the role of mediators as facilitators who can cross boundaries between generations and between professional agencies and local communities. It also shows how neighbourhood, victim-offender and youth mediation work merge in the services offered by a community mediation project.

One of the training projects which focuses on young people has been developed by a Quaker performing arts project as a response to youth unemployment to explore the causes and alternatives to conflict through drama and theatre. Leap Confronting Conflict uses the concept of fire to help to give young people greater understanding of conflict and their feelings about it. Conflict and fire grow in much the same way and though both are dangerous, fire when harnessed can provide warmth and energy. By drama and interactive exercises, youth workers and young people are helped to confront and cope creatively with everyday conflict.

CONCLUSION

This chapter has described some of the innovative conflict resolution work that is being done in schools and with young people. This work is exciting and controversial, but pilot projects have demonstrated the effectiveness of conflict resolution strategies in 'turning a school round' from a culture of bullying in the playground and disorder in the classroom to a culture of participation by the whole school community in the management of the good behaviour in the school.

The work of QPEP in Northern Ireland and the continuing action research work of the EMU Promoting School Project demonstrate the benefits that peer mediation can achieve for the children and school especially within a consistent power-sharing whole school ethos. Northern Ireland experience has shown that the notion of peaceful ways to resolve conflict can also influence behaviour in the adult school community and even the community outside the school. School and project staff have been asked to act as mediators and intermediaries in local disputes and have been able to refer disputes to the Mediation Network Northern Ireland.

Highly publicised cases of violence in schools in mainland Britain have emphasised that existing strategies are not always the answer and a range of alternative mechanisms for resolving conflict could help in the search for ways forward. The work at Highfield Junior School in promoting positive behaviour has changed the school into one of excellence within a few short years. Peer mediation and the empowerment of young people to set their own rules and manage their own conflicts has been demonstrated to be an effective strategy on which to build non-confrontational, co-operative relationships within schools. The success of some conflict resolution projects involving young people suggests that this is a field which merits more work.

SOURCES AND FURTHER READING: *Chapter 7*

Carpenter, V., 'Tackling Bullying', *Safety Education*, ROSPA, Autumn 1993

Cohen, R., *Students Resolving Conflict*, 1995

Fine, N., and Macbeth, F., *Playing With Fire: Training for the Creative Use of Conflict*, 1990

Highfield Junior School, Plymouth and Alderson, P. (Ed.) : *Changing Our School: Promoting Positive Behaviour*, 1997

Kingston Friends Workshop Groups: *Ways and Means: An Approach to Problem Solving*, 1990

Liebmann, M., (Ed.), *Arts Approaches to Conflict*, 1996

Richardson, N., (School of Education, The Queen's Univeristy, Belfast), 'Education for a Divided Society: Mutual Understanding in Northern Ireland's Schools.' Paper present to educationalists in the United States, October 1996

'Rule 1: We Make the Rules', *Daily Telegraph*, 19 February 1997

Smith, A., and Robinson, A., *Education for Mutual Understanding: The Initial Statutory Years*, 1996

Tyrrell, J., *The Quaker Peace Education Project 1988-1994; Developing Untried Strategies*, 1995

Tyrrell, J. and Farrell, S., *Peer Mediation in Primary Schools*, 1995.

Acknowledgments

Society of Friends: Quakers Peace and Service Education Advisory Programme

Kingston Friends Workshop

Centre for Conflict Resolution, University of Ulster.

The Education for Mutual Understanding and Promoting School Project, Northern Ireland
Oakgrove Integrated Primary School, Derry
Ballysally Primary School, Coleraine
Bully-Free Zone, Bolton
National Coalition Building Institute UK
Maidstone Mediation Service
Newham Conflict and Change
Highfield Junior School, Plymouth
The Leaveners/Leap Confronting Conflict Project
Sandwell Mediation Service
Brixton Youth Activities Unit.

CHAPTER 8

Cross-Cultural and Multi-Faith Mediation

New evidence uncovered last week which suggests that the original investigation into Bloody Sunday was seriously prejudiced has been welcomed . . . If the British Government has any interest in peace and trust between communities and between these two islands they should now have the courage and decency to apologise for what was done in their name all those years ago.

The Derry Journal, 21 January 1997

Speaking after loyalist involvement in the Stormont peace talks was guaranteed for now, the Northern Ireland Secretary launched an attack on the Provisionals which used aggressive language and which was being read as a further sign that the security situation in Ulster may be about to deteriorate further . . . 'We will pursue you with every means open to under the law. We shall never give up . . . You will never be safe . . .'

The Guardian, 28 January 1997

The intercultural mediator must know both the values of the disputants as well as his or her own values in depth in order to facilitate meeting and the bonding of new meanings in creating relationships.

Augsburger, *Conflict Mediation Across Cultures*

Our vision is a global community in which people are nurtured and empowered to value differences and to experience conflict as an opportunity for change.

Newham Conflict and Change Vision Statement

A great many agencies in different parts of the world are working to make peace or keep peace in inter-cultural and inter-faith conflicts or to raise mutual awareness and understanding between cultures and faiths so that future conflict may be prevented. The limited aim of this chapter is not to attempt a complete survey nor to explore in detail the complex nature of conflict across different cultures but to examine a few agencies and projects as examples of the work of conflict resolution in this field. Information provided in questionnaires (*Chapter 3*) has been enriched by literature provided by the projects and by follow-up visits and in-depth interviews.

CROSS-CULTURAL MEDIATION

Augsburger reflects that conflict is at one and the same time universal, cultural and individual: it is part of universal human experience; its rules and norms are particular within different cultural settings; to the individual in conflict, his or her situation is unique. Augsburger points out that mediating within one's own culture is complex and confusing enough; mediating in conflicts across more than one culture can lead to total frustration and at worst disaster.

The mediator can first focus on what is universal in conflict. A dispute between neighbours in a quiet suburban street arises from misunderstanding, suspicion, fear, anger and hurt, a range of emotions in response to the perceived threat of attitudes and behaviours. Neighbour is invading the personal space of neighbour by what are interpreted as hostile and aggressive actions or declarations—the barking of a dog, the moving of a boundary stone, an overhanging tree, the parking of a car, the intrusion of a child's game. Confrontational responses arouse feelings of aggression and dispute can escalate into conflict.

If the neighbours are of different cultural backgrounds, the signals sent to and fro are rooted in the traditions and beliefs of each culture and so can be open to misunderstanding and misinterpretation each by the other. To each of the disputants, the conflict is intensely personal, expressed through his or her unique life experience. If such a dispute is brought to a local community mediation service, a mediator from each of the cultural traditions involved would jointly have the knowledge and insight to empathise with both the parties and hopefully the skills to facilitate communication and mutual understanding. Awareness of the significance of such apparently small details as eye contact (which has various, sometimes conflicting, interpretations placed on it by different cultures) or the use of a metaphor may make all the difference in enabling the disputants to establish mutual trust.

East London

A conflict mediation service in East London has been offering neighbourhood mediation services to the local community for 13 years. The workers estimate that there must be at least 50 different cultural traditions represented in the area that the project services. Neighbours are almost bound to come from different cultural groups which means that all the project's mediation work involves cross-cultural issues. The large force of 40 active volunteers, who come from many of the local cultural groups, are trained in cross-cultural awareness so that they are able to help disputants both from their own and other communities to overcome cultural barriers.

CASE STUDY

A typical case, described by a project officer, illustrates the mediation process in a dispute involving cross-cultural issues:

Mr Krishnan, an elderly Sri Lankan, came to the project complaining about the noise that came from his neighbours' household. He claimed that it would usually start at about 9 p.m. often go on until 2 or 3 a.m. He said most of the noise seemed to come from his neighbours' children, and that the youngest, about two years old, seemed to cry a lot. Mr Krishnan, a Hindu, said that in addition to English, he also spoke Gujerati, Hindi and Urdu.

He said he was also bothered by slamming doors, hammering on the walls and loud conversations. He said that sometimes the noise got so bad after he had gone to bed that he would have to get up and go downstairs to watch TV until the noise from next door subsided. He also disclosed that he suffers from a stomach complaint and that his wife has diabetes; the health of both was affected as well as disturbing their sleep patterns.

He said he thought his neighbours were Bengali Muslims. We arranged for two experienced conciliators to visit both families and took the opportunity to send a trainee conciliator who also spoke Syleti.

When our conciliators called on him he retold his story and emphasized the effect on his health. He also said that he had tried speaking to his neighbours several times, requesting that they keep quiet at night. He claimed that they either ignored him or just said OK. When the noise got bad, he would knock back on the wall which would keep the noise down for a while, but it would start again soon after. He had called the police on a couple of but they had simply requested that both parties maintain the peace.

Our conciliators then visited the neighbours; Mr Miah and his family. Mr Miah's English was not very good and so he spoke through his daughter; our Syleti-speaking volunteer was also able to offer assistance. His daughter agreed about the noise and said that the youngest child couldn't go to sleep unless his mother did also. It was the period of Ramadan and the mother was very busy, getting up in the early hours of the morning to prepare food and to eat. It was felt that Mr Krishman was being unreasonable because he would bang on the wall, knock on their front door after midnight, and had several times called the police. Mr Miah was visibly angry about this. He asked why it was, when he had bought his own house, that his children couldn't do what they wanted.

Mr Miah felt that he was being harassed by Mr Krishnan as he and his family had made efforts to keep the noise down by repositioning the TV and putting up thicker wall coverings.

It was disclosed that there was a communication problem between the two households as the elders did not understand one another's languages. Mr Miah said that there were also religious differences which occasionally caused problems. (Mr Miah was uncomplimentary about Hinduism.)

Both parties agreed to enter into mediation as a way of trying to resolve differences between them. The mediation was attended by Mr Krishnan and Mrs Enessa Miah and her daughter Fatima. The Miah's also brought with them the youngest son, Mo, whom Mr Krishnan had said kept him awake with his crying.

As the mediation progressed it became clear that Mr Krishman was keen to maintain friendly relations with his neighbours, but he remained concerned about the noise. Mrs Miah said that they were anxious to avoid upsetting Mr Krishnan and wanted to remain good neighbours, but there was bound to be some noise from her seven children and Mo had been very ill for the last few months and that had made him cry even more.

There had been particular problems around Ramadan because Mrs Miah was cooking late into the night and the family could only eat at certain times. This meant that there might be more noise during this period. Directly related to this was the fact that Mo will only go to sleep when his mother does and therefore his sleep patterns were being disturbed.

Both parties were asked what they would like to see happen in order to make things better. They both firmly stated that they wanted to remain as good neighbours and for normal relations to exist between them. They were then invited to explore ways in which this could happen. Mr Krishnan said that he accepted that the Miah's were doing all they could and hadn't realised that the little boy had been so ill. He said he would try to be more tolerant in the future. He would not bang on the walls and he undertook not to call the police again. Fatima said that in three months' time Mo would be starting at day nursery and would be much more tired in the evenings. Also Ramadan would long be over by then and so the household should be back to normal. However, she said that they would continue to make every effort to keep the noise down, especially now they realised that Mr and Mrs Krishnan had not been well. She added that if Mr Krishnan felt that the noise was getting bad again he could come and knock on their door to let them know.

Both parties were given a written agreement to sign and both went off not only with a better understanding but also with a framework for future relations.

The details of this case include many of the familiar features of neighbour disputes—disturbance of a household by noise from next door; disturbance of elderly people by children; lack of solid, soundproofed party walls making the noise problem difficult to overcome. The situation between these two families was made more difficult because of differences in culture, religion and language. Communication between the heads of the households was prevented by lack of effective common language, and religious and cultural barriers hindered a spontaneous relationship between the womenfolk of the families. Some lack of respect and understanding of each other's religious observances further reduced the tolerance that each side was willing to extend to the other. Mediation by conciliators sensitive to these cross-cultural currents, together with the assistance of an interpreter, allowed communication to flow, from which followed greater understanding and a resolve to build a better relationship. The key to the success of this cross-cultural mediation was the willingness of both sides to use the services of the conciliator to bring them together to discuss their problems.

Many urban areas in the UK now have populations from a rich variety of cultures and mediation services are responding to the diversity of needs in their communities. The worker in the East London service has observed—from her experience—conflict resolution models from different cultures. She feels that while mediation is one way of resolving disputes there is much to be learnt from studying healing relationships in other cultures. Conflict between warring ethnic or sectarian groups or between nations is in essence no different from that between warring neighbours. The causes and emotions are similar, though clearly on a different scale and carrying different levels of destructive potential. When sectarian conflict destroys the peace of whole countries by its violence and bloodshed, the difficulty and the urgency of the peacemaker's task are intensified. The process of achieving peace depends on the mediators' depth of knowledge and understanding of the cultural traditions of the participants.

The Northern Ireland conflict

The conflict in Northern Ireland combines both cross-cultural and religious conflict. The communities are divided by religion and culture and by hundreds of years of history. The walls of Derry are eloquent with one episode in that history. Built in the early seventeenth century to protect the new protestant settlers from London (hence Londonderry) from the surrounding catholic population, they withstood a siege of 105 days in 1689, defending the protestants from the invading armies of catholic James II and his French allies. This contributed to the frustration of James II's attempt to regain the English throne after his expulsion and the accession of William of Orange[1] and Mary in the 'Glorious Revolution' of 1688. As an event in British history, most people in mainland Britain would have to struggle to remember the dates, causes, consequences and significance of what happened. In Derry as in the rest of Northern Ireland it is a present reality and is

---

[1] A small county in the Netherlands, from which the Orange Order gets its name

relived each year on the anniversaries of the significant dates in the calendar by marches and counter-marches. The triumph of the ancestors of one community and the defeat of the ancestors of the other has been confirmed in the succeeding 300 years by British (protestant) colonial rule of (catholic) Ireland, the partition of Ireland in 1921 into the republic of Ireland and Ulster and the recent 30 years of 'the troubles'. In Derry, the protestant minority community until recent years held local political power and the police are perceived by the majority catholic community to be a sectarian security force supported by the British army. The communities live in different parts of the city, organized, supported and terrorised by their paramilitary organizations. The police stay mostly in their armour-plated Land Rovers when they patrol the catholic Bogside, the site of the peaceful civil rights demonstration against internment in 1972 which turned into the massacre of Bloody Sunday.

In this world of conflict, characterised by violence, pain, tension and mistrust, many mediators attempt to build bridges across the sectarian divide, to heal deep historical wounds, to facilitate dialogue and to create mutual understanding of each cultural tradition by the other. One example of a local initiative is the Peace and Reconciliation Group which works in Derry as an intermediary service, defusing rather than resolving conflict. It has contacts with all parties and agencies, including the police, the army and the paramilitaries of both communities, and has succeeded in keeping open channels of communication because it is respected as a voluntary organization having no vested interest in the outcome of particular conflict situations.

Following incidents of violence between communities, or between one community and the security forces, they can talk with both sides to defuse a potentially explosive situation and to build bridges to prevent the widening of the divide. This work is defined in two of the group's objectives:

> To provide an essential intermediary and liaison role with and between polarised sections and institutions of the community.
> To narrow the gap between the security forces and the community by facilitating an open channel of communication until there is an acceptable and agreed police service.

After the breakdown of the ceasefire in February 1996, the army resumed its street patrols and the police service remained unacceptable to many in both communities. The focus of the group's work is now concerned with intra-community conflict in situations where paramilitary organizations are imposing 'discipline' within their communities by intimidation, beatings, arson attacks and murders of those who are allegedly guilty of anti-social behaviour.

> A mother in great distress came to seek the help of the group. Her son aged 19 had been charged by the police with a petrol bombing. Three others had subsequently also been charged and loyalist paramilitaries say that her son informed on them. He is being used as a scapegoat in the situation and his life is in danger. He is now out on bail and has to appear in court in two weeks' time. The Group is now trying to move him to a place of safety and are waiting to hear from the loyalists if he would be safe in the short term in a house in Belfast.

The Peace and Reconciliation Group is initiating a three-year action plan to provide a community mediation service with the aim of offering to both communities a third option, an alternative to either police or paramilitaries, for solving neighbourhood disputes. Working with the Mediation Network for Northern Ireland, they will recruit and train volunteers from local communities who will be available to mediate in disputes and who will also work proactively with young people at risk of being targeted for anti-social behaviour. The key to the success of this service will be its credibility, which will depend on the involvement of key local people who will embrace within the mediation process the cultural traditions of the community. This mediation service will meet other objectives of the project:

- to promote reconciliation effectively in a community relations and community context
- to continue to reduce tension at grass roots level
- to provide a mediation service to individuals, groups or institutions which concentrates on themes and issues relating to the conflict, sectarianism or cultural identity.

The Peace and Reconciliation Group recognises that the conflict transformation period of the peace process is still to come in Northern Ireland. Communities will be more willing to engage in cross community reconciliation processes when they can accept with confidence an agreed political framework. The Women's Coalition is working to resolve the ethnic and cultural conflicts in Northern Ireland by the achievement of that agreed political framework.

The Women's Coalition
Women in the Coalition are working to resolve cultural conflict on two fronts simultaneously and finding the task tough and demanding. On the one hand, they are struggling within a gender conflict to gain

acceptance of the right of women to play an equal part in political life. Women traditionally have been allowed little political voice in the 'tribal' (their label) politics of Northern Ireland. There are no women MPs representing Northern Ireland constituencies at Westminster. Only 12 per cent of local councillors are women. Fifty per cent of local councils have no female members at all. Four of the 17 councillors on Derry City Council are women. When the elections for the all party talks were proposed, women who believed that women's voices should be heard had to decide whether to try to work their way into the traditional parties, from whom direct approaches produced little or no response, or to form their own party. Supported by experience in the European Women's Lobby, the Women's Coalition was formed and successfully campaigned to gain representation at the talks.

The Women's Coalition includes members from all religions and all traditional political alignments. They will talk with anyone on any issues and hold 'a strong mediation philosophy'. Because they represent all parties, they hold no fixed position on constitutional issues and are ready to negotiate around innovative ideas. Their manifesto statements make their position clear:

> Traditional political parties will bring their fixed agendas on the constitutional question to negotiation; the Women's Coalition is dedicated to drawing together the different views, ideas and options to achieve a workable solution. Over the years of violence women have been very effective in developing and maintaining contact across the various divides in our society. They have created a space for discussion and for an honest exchange of views. In doing this women have seen themselves as agents of change. The search for solutions needs a sense of openness and willingness to talk, not confrontation and hidden agendas.
>
> The N. I. Women's Coalition is prepared to help in the negotiation of a political accommodation which takes account of all sides of the key divisions in Northern Ireland and allows for cultural and political diversity building a multi-cultural, multi-ethnic and multi-religious society. The N. I. Women's Coalition is prepared to work to secure agreement across all interests and all parties for a workable solution.

The Women's Coalition does not hold that women necessarily can make a better contribution to finding solutions but they do believe that women can contribute a more informed approach because from their long experience of oppression they know more about how to seek compromise rather than confrontation. They have made strong statements on issues of Equity and Human Rights, from which these are extracts:

The need for a politics and a society based on the principle of Equity is seen as crucial by the Northern Ireland Women's Coalition. The vast majority of women have lost out in terms of economic, social and political power and it is important that this fact is acknowledged and that clear strategies to promote women's inclusion are identified and adopted. As a first step all economic, social and political policies must be gender-proofed, in order to assess their possible differential impact on men and women; and all political parties should integrate a gender perspective into all their policies.

Respect for Human Rights must be of concern to all who are living here irrespective of political allegiance and must be the cornerstone of any credible peace process if we are to move towards a more pluralist and just society. Only by building a settlement on the foundation of Human Rights can we hope to build a new and peaceful society, where all are treated with respect, and where equality of treatment is guaranteed.

The women's perspective adds a different dimension to the debate on many crucial issues; for example, their recommendations on political prisoners focus on social deprivation, the hardship suffered by families and the rights of victims in contrast to the male perspective on all sides which is more militaristic. The women representatives have faced a challenging time but have been determined to hold their own space at the talks table and claim the right to participate in discussion on all issues. They have been bullied, shouted at and physically jostled as well as ridiculed for their deliberate flexibility on constitutional issues, but they believe that they are slowly changing the norms of political behaviour in Northern Ireland and undermining by erosion the cultural dominance of perceived tribal politics. They are in the political arena to stay and it will no longer be possible to dismiss women and children as not having a voice in the context of what they do.

Multi-faith peacemaking in Ireland
Religious traditions are at the centre of the conflict in Northern Ireland so they have to be part of the solution. Many religious leaders (and non-leaders) in Northern Ireland are working for peace, working discreetly and with confidentiality to break down the barriers between the communities. Initiatives at local level often emerge from *non-leaders* who are less strongly focused on orthodoxy and the well-being of their institution. The International Institute of Peace Studies and Global Philosophy with the Ireland group of the World Conference on Religion and Peace brought together representatives of all spiritual traditions and faiths in Ireland in June 1997 'to discuss the paths to peace and non-violence through interfaith understanding, tolerance, diversity and the role of education, prayer and spirituality in changing entrenched mind sets and tackling the many problems of contemporary Irish society'. This brought together the Institute, the World Conference on Religion

and Peace, the School of Non-violence and Conflict Resolution and the Multifaith and Multicultural Mediation Service, in all of which Dr. Thomas Daffern is actively engaged. He is working as an inter-faith mediator trying to bring all religions together globally and in particular in the context of the Northern Ireland conflict. He feels that peacemaking has become too secular in approach and that the spiritual content to conflict resolution is being overlooked. Peacemaking needs to be addressed at spiritual depth; religious communities are a powerful forum for promoting peace and though the work of bringing them together as a united force is difficult, slow and sometimes frustrating, the shift of energy that such a forum brings about has enormous potential for bringing about the miracle of peace. People of faith and spirituality are working to enable religious communities to become what they claim to be. The vision of this approach may hold out more hope for the future than the search for a political solution.

As well as the efforts of individuals in their parishes, catholics and protestants work together formally in schools and communities in the Churches' Peace Education Programme. The hard work for peace by religious groups rarely makes headlines in the news as it lacks the sensation and drama of violence.

Issues arising from the cultural conflict in Northern Ireland

Many common observations can be made about the conflict in Northern Ireland and ethnic conflicts in other parts of the world. Cultural conflict can be confronted by the use of force or by what is termed 'clout' mediation, or by emergency bridge-building, but such intervention achieves at best a *short term* defusion of the conflict situation. Resolution of an ethnic conflict is not possible when the attitudes and behaviour patterns are so entrenched in history and tradition that the aspirations of the two sides are incompatible and the differences between them irreconcilable.

Augsburger suggests that in such conflicts, transformation of attitudes and behaviour should be the goal of the culturally sensitive mediator. The mediator's task, working from his or her understanding of the cultural sensitivities, is to separate attitudes and behaviour of people from the conflict situation and enable people to discover mutual respect and trust, and from these new positions develop collaborative and co-operative ways of working and living side by side. In Lederach's terms, 'The model is not transferred; it is created. It is not prescriptive; it is elicitive.' Mediators who come from within the conflict and have themselves experienced conflict transformation are much more credible than outsiders. The potential for harnessing spiritual energy in the peacemaking process is being explored by multi-faith mediators and by representatives of all churches and religious communities.

Within an ethnic conflict, other less visible struggles may be taking place such as the gender conflict in which the Women's Coalition is engaged: 'Inclusion is not only about protestant and catholic—it is about gender too'. Outcomes can only be reached by small steps, building on small gains in trust and mutual respect, and the process is most likely to be fruitful if an acceptable overarching political framework is in place or is perceived to be under construction.

Other peace work by faiths

Most religious denominations and faiths have organizations within them which are dedicated to the pursuit of peace such as the Buddhist Peace Fellowship and the Catholic Pax Christi. They do, however, each stress the advantages of their own particular path to peace and work mainly within their own following which is why multi-faith organizations and multi-faith mediators are needed. The World Conference on Religion and Peace (UK and Ireland Group) is one of 80 member organizations of the Inter-faith Network for the UK which aims to build good relationships between people of different faiths in Britain.

Some religious groups combine networking and peace education with practical peacemaking; notable among these is the Religious Society of Friends. For 300 years the Quakers have practised their belief that violence and war are always wrong by promoting peace and peaceful ways of resolving conflict. Quaker Peace and Service (QPS) operates internationally through projects working persistently and quietly for peace and justice in many of the most troubled countries in the world, notably Sri Lanka, the Middle East and the former Soviet Union. Quakers are also active peacemakers in Northern Ireland, working in all communities through projects such as the QPEP initiative described in *Chapter 7*.

As well as offering political mediation at a governmental level, QPS works at community-level peacebuilding with conciliation programmes aimed at repairing the consequences of violence in local communities 'through humanitarian work and the provision of training in non-violent conflict resolution.'

Bridge Builders
Bridge Builders is a mediation service for all Christian denominations and churches provided by the London Mennonite Centre. Their mediators will work with congregations who are experiencing difficulties using strategies common to all situations where mediation is appropriate.

In some cases of church conflict, mediation will be an appropriate way to transform the situation; for example, where a congregation is developing into two major factions with unsatisfactory dialogue between them. Mediation is particularly appropriate in situations where the issue is important to the congregation, and when trust has begun to break down.

Bridge Builders' mediators empower groups to identity their own solutions which will meet the needs of all parties in the dispute.

NCBI
The National Coalition Building Institute (NCBI) is not based on a particular faith but aims to work creatively with prejudice and conflict to bring together people of all faiths and cultures. Its leaders reflect the cultures in the communities it works in; for example, two thirds of the leaders in NCBI in America are from African, Asian, Jewish or Latino cultural roots while the leadership in UK reflects proportionally the main faiths and cultures of British society.

CONCLUSION

This chapter has examined conflicts in which misunderstanding, misconceptions and historical antagonisms continue to divide cultures and faiths. Conflicts with roots in contrasting or competing ideological and cultural traditions are among the most intractable to solve. Deep felt prejudice has to be confronted and acknowledged and a culture of hatred, revenge, violence and fear has to undergo transformation into a culture of tolerance, mutual trust and respect and non-violence in order for peacemaking processes to succeed and peace to be permanent. The voices of those involved in efforts to effect transformation in one conflict have resonance with other comparable conflicts. All conflicts are universal, cultural and individual as are the skills, knowledge and understanding required by mediators to transform them creatively into positive situations with hope for peace.

SOURCES AND FURTHER READING: *Chapter 8*

Augsburger, D. A., *Conflict Mediation Across Cultures: Pathways and Patterns, 1992*
Lederach, J. P., *Preparing for Peace: Conflict Transformation Across Cultures, 1995.*

Acknowledgments
Newham Conflict and Change
Centre for Conflict Resolution, University of Ulster

Peace and Reconciliation Group, Derry
The Women's Coalition
The Women's Centre, Derry
Dr. Thomas Daffern, International Institute of Peace Studies and Global Philosophy
Bridge Builders, London Mennonite Centre
National Coalition Building Institute, UK
Quaker Peace Service.

CHAPTER 9

Environmental Conflict

WORLD HEADS FOR DISASTER

World demand for water is doubling every 21 years. The consensus of scientists is that man-induced climate change has started. If carbon dioxide in the atmosphere doubles, as it will within two generations, 36 countries may be covered in water and 100 million people will have to move. Ozone losses over mid to high latitudes have increased rapidly as have ultra violet radiation from Chile, to Russia, the USA and Britain. By the year 2000 there will be 6.5 billion people on earth, up 58 per cent since 1950. The world population grows by more than 88 million a year.

The Guardian, 28 January 1997

These are just some of the ways, according to *The Guardian* report, in which 'Irresponsible and shortsighted governments are pushing the world rapidly towards environmental and economic disaster.' Environmental conflict is perhaps the biggest issue of current conflict in the world. The threat to world ecosystems from global warming, holes in the ozone layer and acid rain are presented forcefully and regularly to us by scientists and environmental organizations. We read and believe in the threat to life on this planet and then get the car out to drive to the supermarket. There is unresolved conflict between our use of the earth and its resources and the long term sustainability of earth as a habitable planet.

Environmental conflicts and their resolution are not new. For example in the seventeenth century fen drainage and land reclamation was good for landowners but caused silting up of the upper reaches of the River Cam and disaster to the livelihood of watermen and merchants in Cambridge. In 1702 the Conservators of the River Cam were set up by an Act of Parliament to keep the river navigable through Cambridge and to resolve disputes between riverside landowners and watermen. The elements of this historic dispute are common to all environmental conflict—issues of access and issues of impact and how to reconcile accessibility to the world's resources with economic, environmental and social sustainability.

A note on sources of information

No questionnaire respondents (*Chapter 3*) indicated that they were working in the field of environmental conflict. The four environmental organizations listed in the Mediation UK Directory were contacted and useful information obtained. Helpful and valuable information was also provided by Dr. Roger Sidaway, an active and experienced environmental mediator from the Institute of Ecology and Resource Management at Edinburgh University. Current environmental issues have been used as examples and case studies.

CASE STUDY

Environmental conflicts were played out on a small scale at a conference in January 1997 organized by the Countryside Recreation Network on Access to Water. The conference brought together representatives of leisure groups who need access to water for their activities, conservationists, water companies and riparian interests. One purpose of the conference was to allow parties to air their grievances and perhaps to lay the groundwork for resolving them.

The two main issues under discussion were the right of access to water for recreational use and the impact on water resources of increased use by different groups of users. The right of access to the 84,000 hectares of inland water and the linear waterways in England and Wales is an area of dispute between anglers and canoeists. In law, owners of land on river banks extend their ownership to the midway point in the river. Navigation rights exist in common law only if the river has been in use as a navigable waterway since time immemorial. Two million plus fresh water anglers pay licence fees to landowners for the right to fish their rivers. They feel that they both pay for their sport and keep the law. As there is no right of navigation on most rivers and anyone landing on privately-owned river banks without permission is trespassing, the 100,000 canoeists, who want to be able to travel the length of any river to pursue their sport, break the law, trespass when they land on river banks and come into conflict with the anglers whose sport is disrupted by their passage. To anglers, canoeists are both lawbreakers and freeriders.

Passions and prejudice ran high at the conference. Positions polarised and it was clear that conflict was likely to escalate unless some formula for co-existence and compromise could be negotiated. Other parties involved in access—landowners, the sports council and water authorities—and those concerned about impact—conservationists and the Environment Agency—are all concerned about the overall increase in leisure use of water resources. Conflict of interest between water authorities, industrial users of water, farmers and conservationists underlay the vociferous dispute between the two leisure users. Concern at the environmental impact of increased demand from all users on a resource diminishing because of lower levels of rainfall brought calls for the setting up of a water access forum on which all interested groups would be represented with a brief to draw up a national plan, to mediate local solutions of disputes and to research the best policy and practice for future management. Everyone agreed that more communication between the different interests would go a long way to defusing conflict in the future.

Progress was made towards resolving the conflict between the anglers and the canoeists. The two parties at least listened to each other's story for the first time. Each said that the other's attitude was confrontational; canoeists accused anglers of refusing to talk with them and anglers spoke bitterly of the canoeists' blatant trespassing. Having heard each other's case, both sides expressed willingness to sit down and negotiate, possibly with a mediator, and probably on a river by river basis. The representative of the Country Landowners Association (hardly neutral as farmers stand to gain licence fees from leisure users) offered their services as mediators between the interests in the hope that a shared-use agreement could get both sides more or less what they wanted. All parties agreed that the over-riding aim must be environmental sustainability. The conference was an excellent example of how the sharing of information, frank and full communication, mutal understanding of different points of view and the acceptance of the principle of mediation can pave the way for resolving a long-running dispute.

Participatory planning and mediation

The Access to Water conference illustrated clearly two developing strategies for handing conflict in the environment. Participatory planning is a way of consensus building to prevent conflict in the environmental field and mediation is developing to resolve conflict between interests in dispute. Both approaches are provided by Environmental Resolve, an undertaking of the independent Environment Council, a charity dedicated to protecting and enhancing the quality and diversity of Britain's environment for present and future generations. 'Environmental Resolve aims to realise sustainability by working with interest groups to find and implement practical solutions to shared environmental issues and opportunities.'

Environmental Resolve points out that the process of public enquiry about planning issues, while giving local people the opportunity to be involved in the decision-making process, in fact encourages and polarises conflict because of its adversarial approach. Dr. Sidaway agrees that 'Public consultation may be no more than the dissemination of information, good public relations or tokenism which aims at placating the public and which make little contribution to conflict resolution'. The strong feelings expressed by road protesters and the violence which receives so much publicity between the protesters and security guards and police usually burst out after a public enquiry has been completed, demonstrating that many people do not accept the process as a legitimate or inclusive way of making decisions. The creation and implementation of public order and 'anti-social behaviour' legislation—can criminalises protesters—and further exacerbates the situation, emphasising the urgency of looking for new approaches.

Environmental Resolve works through consensus building which brings together interest groups or stakeholders involved in a situation with a mediator to facilitate discussion and assist the framing of an agreed solution. Dr. Sidaway comments:

> The consensus building approach to planning problems is based on the philosophy of planning *with* people rather than *for* them. In which case the role of professionals is to listen and advise so that they enable people to make the decision rather than deciding for them. The emphasis is on encouraging full public involvement in planning decisions. There are important distinctions between *consultation* and *public involvement* which revolve around whether the public is an equal party in the planning exercise and the timing of public participation.

The mediator assists the stakeholders to find ways of working together effectively, to clarify issues, to form alliances and collaborate in the formulation of solutions. The process culminates in commitment to implement agreed plans of action. Dr. Sidaway points out that a limitation to the effectiveness of consensus building or mediation in environmental issues is the imbalance in the power of the stakeholder interests involved:

> The success of mediation depends mainly on the willingness of the parties to enter negotiation and this is unlikely to be the case where one party is markedly more powerful than the other. It is clear that voluntary negotiations will not solve problems arising from a radically unbalanced distribution of power . . . A reluctance to share power may inhibit the wider applications of consensus building. It is worth noting that the aim of most government agencies is to execute some aspect of public policy and as a result few are politically neutral . . . There is the risk that during informal process of consensus building, weaker parties may be at a disadvantage and that their basic rights may not be safeguarded.

He suggests that in Britain consensus building may be a useful supplement to conventional procedures. He notes that the procedures for environmental mediation are better developed in the United States but cites the example of negotiations within the Access Consultative

Group in the Peak District National Park as an example of use of the process in Britain. The conflict over public access to open moorland in the Peak Park was addressed by an alternative strategy in the early 1990s, as a committee report outlines:

> There has been a long history of tension and conflicts over such access. The alternative to conflict is to see whether competing interests can be reconciled by preparing a plan which concentrates on public access issues. Such a plan would consider how access might be secured and extended throughout the moorland areas without interfering with the legitimate activities of landowners, farmers and sporting occupiers or with the interests of wildlife.

Consensus building was the key to the success of the alternative strategy. Following an analysis of its access strategy—*Access to Open Country: A Balanced Approach*—the National Park established an Access Consultative Group to bring together representatives of the landowners, conservationists and recreational interests to discuss concerns and plan a co-operative way forward. Assisted by an independent facilitator, the Group met seven times over a period of nine months. At these meetings, each interest was able to express feelings and needs on an equal footing, and common ground could be established. Starting from entrenched positions of hostility and mutual suspicion, as the meetings progressed trust, goodwill, openness and a willingness to listen to each other's points of view developed. The interests of conservationists in establishing more sanctuary areas of restricted access to protect endangered species such as the golden plover were balanced by an understanding by the landowners of the need to open additional areas to public access in return for agreed good management practices to address concerns about, for example, erosion and the disturbance of sheep. In this way, each interest felt that they had gained while the common interest of conserving the natural resource of the moorlands for future generations was recognised. A commitment was made by all participants to the preparation of collaborative local Access Management Plans and future involvement in the process:

> The Access Management Group suggests that its future role might be to review the programme of Access Management Planning, to review progress in preparing individual plans and to consider the effectiveness of this approach to planning and the negotiation of new access . . . It is unlikely that each member of the AMG will be able to take part in the preparation of individual Access Management Plans in which case they would nominate representatives to ensure that local knowledge of their interest is incorporated in the plans.

The consensus building process in the Peak Park has therefore both addressed the long-running conflict by developing dialogue and common ground between the stakeholders and laid a foundation for the prevention of conflict in the future by planning for ongoing consultation and collaboration. Dr. Sidaway looks to consensus building on the Peak Park model as the way such conflicts over access, conservation and the local economy can be addressed in the future.[1]

Examples given by Environmental Resolve of other consensus building programmes include planning the development of a central area in Bristol, working with the British Wind Energy Association to produce guidelines for the development of wind energy, and solving the problem of disposal of waste in Hampshire. Environmental Resolve's mediators are also involved in the 'Roundtable' of community and environmental interests set up to carry forward locally issues raised at the Rio Earth Summit of 1992 and to plan a sustainable development strategy. The Roundtable initiative is based on Canadian experience where they have become an established part of environmental decision-making. The UK Roundtable has begun to make its voice heard on policy issues. For example, their report in February 1997 highlighted the effects on pollution levels of increased traffic using out-of-town developments as a result of local councils ignoring government guidelines on curbing development on greenfield sites. Also in February 1997 the Roundtable was instrumental in bringing together the interests of environmentalists, consumers, the Forestry Commission and the Timber Growers' Association to join in a Forest Stewardship Council to promote a scheme for awarding certification of good management to timber products that come from well managed forest areas.[2]

The Environmental Law Foundation is an organization which puts local groups in touch with local lawyers who will act on a voluntary basis as case assistants. Assisted by legal expertise, the groups are often able to achieve negotiated settlements in environmental matters.

GLOBAL ENVIRONMENTAL ISSUES

An example of how even a multi-national giant company is beginning to show some environmental concern is given in reports in February

---

[1] A valuable full account and assessment of the Peak negotiations has now been published by Dr. Sidaway. In 1998, the Labour government announced a policy initiative towards encouraging a voluntary open access policy to land suitable for recreation.

[2] The Environmental Council, *Beyond Compromise: Building Consensus in Environmental Planning and Decision-making.*

1997 of Shell's plans to meet the concerns of its critics. Shell came under sharp attack for its plans to dump the Brent Spar oil rig in the Atlantic Ocean, for its environmental damage to the Ogoni region of Nigeria and its role in the conflict between the Nigerian government and local protesters and for its general environmental awareness. Although it is committed to the principal of sustainability, in practice its extraction and exploration of new sources of fossil fuels continues unabated. Under pressure from consumers whose boycotts of its petrol stations hit Shell where it hurts, Shell is attempting to change its image. A Shell spokesman told a Dutch audience 'We have discovered that we have to place a new emphasis on listening and exchanging views. We have found we have to communicate more—internally and externally.' And an acknowledgement of the possibility of limits to oil exploitation came in a contribution to a public forum in November:

> It does seem increasingly probably that man-made carbon dioxide, largely from fossil fuels, may affect climate—albeit much less than in previous projections based on an unrealistic view of how energy markets could develop next century.

The hope for the environmental mediator in this report lies in the evidence that even a multi-national company is finding that it is in its own interests to listen to and perhaps in the end to negotiate with other stakeholders to find common ground on which to build a more sustainable world future. There is hope that the voices of those with little power as individuals may be able to find ways of being heard even by the big corporations. The First Nation people in American have little political or economic power but speak with a deep spiritual vision and authority of 'loving the land' which belonged to their fathers' fathers. The moral force of such vision is perhaps shared by the German housewives who protested in the face of massed armed troops against the storage of nuclear waste in their locality.

A final case study illustrates the complex interface between conservation and international relations expressed in the Common Fisheries Policy of the European Community. The following account of some recent work of the Fisheries Commission has been supplied by one of its permanent officers.

The Common Fisheries Policy of the European Community: A Case Study in Conflict Resolution[3]

Whether it was simply the expression of the determination of the then Member States to defend their fish stocks and fishing rights in common at the time of the generalised extension of Exclusive Economic Zones by the World's coastal states in 1976, or whether it also reflected the desire of the minor Community Member States to harness the resources of the major fishing States, the United Kingdom and Denmark, the Common Fisheries Policy (CFP) remains an interesting paradigm of conflict resolution at the international level.

These conflicts are many at the economic, environmental, social and political level. Indeed, given the national emotions stirred by fisheries issues in all Community seafaring Member States, it is remarkable that the CFP works as well as it does. If diplomacy is the continuation of war by other means, then that is exactly what happens in the annual Council session in Brussels which sets TACs[4] and quotas for the following year. The fact that this always takes place just a few days before Christmas is of course purely fortuitous.

What is not fortuitous is that the December Council session lasts for two days and one night. This is not because the decisions to be taken in the Community system of checks and balances always concern large amounts of fish - far from it, bitter struggles can take place over less that 100 tonnes of a particular species — or that the number of seafaring nations has increased since the accession of Spain, Portugal, Sweden and Finland, but it is essentially because there are less and less fish, year by year, of many of the main commercial stocks in the North Sea and elsewhere. Thus the December Council is the place and time for the resolution of conflicting interests of the Member States, through, normally, not one but two successive compromise solutions presented by the Presidency to a bleary-eyed Council in the early hours of the morning. There is no point in prolonging the agony, especially with Christmas round the corner.

The Council begins on the basis on the Commission's proposal. The Presidency compromise or compromises have therefore to be endorsed by the Commission, because in the Community system of checks and balances a decision can only be voted in fisheries by a majority if it is supported by the Commission — otherwise the unanimous agreement of all Member States is required, and this is too dangerous a procedure to contemplate. Thus in December 1996 the TACs and quotas for 1997 were adopted by majority vote with Sweden and Belgium voting against. The United Kingdom delegation, which obtained among others the right to kill 370 tonnes more West of Scotland cod, 1,250 tonnes more haddock 1,500 more tonnes of whiting, 50 tonnes more Channel plaice and 35 tonnes more

---

[3] These statements are strictly personal and do not reflect the official views of the Institutions of the European Union in any way.

[4] TAC = Total Allowable Catch

Channel sole than the Commission originally proposed, voted in favour, in the middle of the BSE 'mad cow' crisis. Incidentally, because the Presidency changes every six months, every Member State has a crack at resolving the TACs and quota conflicts each December — the United Kingdom will have to rely on the Austrian Presidency in 1998.

The December Council session is not necessarily restricted entirely to TACs and quotas. In December 1996 there were at least three negotiations going on in parallel through the night, one on TACs and quotas, one on the new satellite surveillance system, and one on the share-out of fishing rights in the Baltic Sea. These negotiations were all designed to resolve the conflicting interests of the Member States and the Commission, the Presidency, of course, remaining neutral.

Behind the actual negotiations in the December Council always lurks the conflict of interests with third countries, in particular Norway, with whom the Community shares the management of important stocks in the North Sea in order to avoid unresolved conflict with Norway. The Commission's proposals themselves are based on the latest scientific advice of the Advisory Committee for Fisheries Management of the International Council for the Exploration of the Sea; this latest scientific advice from the fisheries biologists is commonly challenged by the fishermen in the various Member States who continually lobby their national governments.

The CFP has a much wider ambit than conservation and management of fisheries resources. It covers, among other things, structural policies designed to provide subsidies for the reduction of Community fleets, the development of port facilities, auction installations and so on, where again there will be conflicts of interest between many different protagonists. The common market organization, with its own Community rules and incentives, brings into place the conflicting interests of fishermen, middlemen, fish processors, transport undertakings and ancillary industries, not to mention the consumers. An example of such a conflict is the current importation of Norwegian salmon into the Community market and the recent efforts, made by Scottish and Irish fishermen's organizations, to cause the Commission to impose anti-dumping measures against Norway.

The whole range of the CFP is thus a wide spectrum of conflicting individual and collective interests, all of which try to promote themselves vigorously at the expense of others. It is therefore on balance encouraging to see that all member states and most of their fishing industries concur that the resolution of these many daily conflicts should take place in the context of an agreed system for conflict resolution based on the rule of law.

The countries of the Community will continue to horse-trade the details of conservation of fish stocks and levels of allowable catches of different species of fish. What the mechanisms of the Community provide is a process whereby consensus building and compromise through negotiation, shuttle diplomacy and mediation take place through the agency of the Presidency of the day, in co-operation with the Commission, and assisted by the permanent officials of the Council Secretariat.

EFFECTIVENESS OF MEDIATION

Environmental conflict seems to be more and more reported in the news while consensus-building or mediation receives less publicity. Conflict arises between those interests which demand more access to resources, for leisure use or on grounds of economic development and profit, and those who are seeking to protect the environment from the damaging impact of too much or inappropriate use. The access interests are often more powerful, backed by the big money of international finance, in oil companies, road haulage interests and agri-business, while the impact groups such as road protesters and ramblers have a strong moral appeal but little power. The beginnings of an alliance between the more 'respectable' environmental groups and the Ecowarriors in the protest against the new runway at Manchester Airport may be the beginning of a more powerful lobby whose voice may have influence in the future and hasten a recognition that all interests in the community should be included in environmental planning procedures.

However, the effectiveness of political protest in changing public opinion on, for example, road building policies, may discourage developers from listening to those mediation initiatives which are not backed by violent demonstrations. That mediation in environment disputes is slow to develop in Britain is partly a tribute to the success of the preventative strategies of consensus building. Dr. Sidaway also points out that mediators are slow to evaluate and publish their work in this field which in turn starves organizations of information and appreciation of the possibilities of the mediation process. Without such understanding, campaigning organizations may feel threatened by the risks of power sharing when the balance of power seems so weighted in favour of the developers and professional politicians.[5]

Disputes about access to water for leisure activities pale in significance when set against the global demand for water, and the rights of ramblers and landowners are trivial in the context of the depletion of world forests and the degradation by soil erosion of billions of hectares of land in Africa and Asia. Although mediation and consensus-building strategies are now on the agenda as ways to resolve

---

[5] The points in the paragraph are offered by Dr. Sidaway in a personal communication.

conflict, small gains for environmental sustainability seem more than cancelled out by the accelerating pressure on earth's resources, the impact of which is rapidly becoming irreversible.

SOURCES AND FURTHER READING: *Chapter 9*

Amy, D., *The Politics of Environmental Mediation*, 1987

Elson, M., *Green Belts: Conflict Mediation in the Urban Fringe*, 1986

Environmental Council, The, *Beyond Compromise: Building Consensus in Environmental Planning and Decision-making*, 1995

Peak Park Joint Planning Board, *Access to Open Country: A Balanced Approach, A Draft Strategy*, 1992

Sidaway, R., 'The Use of Consensus Building in Planning and Conflict Resolution: A Brief Introduction to Consensus Building and Mediation Techniques'. A paper prepared for a joint conference of the Countryside Recreation Network and the Landscape Research Group, 19-20 November 1996, Peterborough, CRN, Cardiff

Sidaway, R., *Access Management by Local Consensus: Reducing Environment Impacts by Negotiation*, 1997.

Acknowledgments

Dr. Roger Sidaway, Institute of Ecology and Resource Management, University of Edinburgh

Beth Morgan, The Conservators of the River Cam

John Bishop, Peak National Park

Hywel Duck, Council of the European Union

Countryside Recreation Network

Environmental Resolve

Environmental Law Foundation.

CHAPTER 10

David and Goliath

And there went out a champion out of the camp of the Philistines named Goliath of Gath, whose height was six cubits and a span. And when the Philistine looked about and saw David he disdained him for he was but a youth and ruddy and of fair countenance. And David prevailed over the Philistine with a sling and with a stone and smote the Philistine and slew him.

1 Samuel XVII, vv. 4, 42 and 50

One answer to the problem is a tried, tested and ancient method of dispute resolution — arbitration.

Chartered Institute of Arbitrators

And Solomon said, Divide the living child in two and give half to the one and half to the other.

1 Kings IV, v. 25

To decide how to resolve your dispute, you may find it helpful to think about what you want and what sort of procedure you are prepared to use to get it.

Lord Chancellor's Department

In the story of David and Goliath, the two protagonists are individuals representing their sides in a conflict. Instead of whole armies fighting, champions were chosen to do battle on their behalf and the outcome decided the contest. This was an economical way of resolving a conflict, saving life and preserving honour. Such contests were supposed to be between the best fighters on each side; however no one on the Israelite side could match Goliath in size and strength and it took the subtle strategy of a relatively unarmed and untried shepherd boy to take on the fully armed giant and defeat him. So David has come to symbolise the powerless 'little person' taking on the might and resources of the large body, Goliath—and winning.

This chapter describes and reviews some of the mechanisms that have been developed to assist the 'Davids' to take on the 'Goliaths'. Individuals who have complaints and disputes against government agencies and large organizations rarely have the resources to engage in a costly adversarial battle in the courts. Because of this, the rights of individuals can with impunity be subordinated to the convenience, profit, inertia and bureaucracy of faceless organizations. In a democratic society, this is perceived to be unacceptable, and, in addition to the civil legal framework, mechanisms to redress the balance of power are provided by dispute resolution schemes which assist individuals to match up to the power of the state and the corporate giant.

The story of the judgment of Solomon is a warning to those who bring disputes to outside arbitrators that the decision reached may not always be what they expected or wanted.[1]

RESOLUTION MECHANISMS: DEVELOPMENT

David was prepared to take on Goliath because he believed that his cause was just and because he had previous experience in overcoming bears and lions in defence of his flocks. Many individuals may feel strongly that they have a justifiable reason for complaint but lack the experience and confidence to initiate the dispute. Goliath was out there demanding a champion with whom to do battle; organizations do not look for unhappy customers or clients but deploy resources in preparation for blocking attack. In an American fast food chain, the customer is invited to complain to the management if the waiter fails to smile. In the UK, mechanisms for making complaints are now spelled out by many organizations and agencies, though still sometimes in small print and obscure corners.

The Lord Chancellor's Department issues a clear and informative booklet on *Resolving Disputes Without Going to Court* which summarises many of the various options and schemes available and the advantages and disadvantages of each. As a first option, direct negotiation with an authority or organization may sort out a dispute quickly and cheaply, but if such approaches were always successful there would be no need for other mechanisms. However, approaches to a trade association arbitration scheme or an ombudsman scheme or regulator to get assistance in resolving a dispute require knowledge, time and a high level of organization, as well as persistence and efficiency in assembling the facts of the case. Many people would benefit from the advice of a solicitor or the expertise available in a Law Centre or Citizens' Advice Bureau in order to be able to make an effective application.

Snapshot of work in this field

Responses were received from 16 organizations in this field, ten ombudsmen schemes and six trade or professional associations. The

---

[1] It also identified the real mother of the child who withdrew her claim when faced with such an outcome: hence 'the wisdom of Soloman'.

detailed information provided by many of these respondents has been supplemented by telephone interviews, additional reference material and detailed information from a practitioner in the field.

Arbitration schemes
The Chartered Institute of Arbitrators defines arbitration as:

> A procedure for the settlement of disputes, under which the parties agree to be bound by the decision of an arbitrator, which is, in general, final and legally binding on both parties. It is conducted within a framework of statute law, principally the Arbitration Acts 1950-1979 as amended.

The Arbitration Act 1996 is discussed in relation to its impact on commercial mediation in *Chapter 11*.

Arbitration is the last resort of alternative dispute resolution strategies. When a customer is in dispute about goods or services and cannot get satisfaction from the supplier, the next step—short of legal proceedings—is to check if the supplier belongs to a trade association to which the complaint can be taken. For example, if a dispute about the quality of a package holiday is not settled by the tour operator, it can be pursued through the Association of British Travel Agents. The association will try to arrange a resolution of the dispute which is acceptable to both sides through a process of conciliation. If conciliation is unsuccessful at this level, the dispute can be referred to the services offered by the Chartered Institute of Arbitrators (CIA).

The CIA was founded in 1915, incorporated in 1924, granted a Royal Charter in 1979 and became a charity in 1990. It has 8,000 member organizations from a wide range of professional and commercial fields and provides services 'to promote and facilitate the determination of disputes by arbitration'. As well as working with its member bodies to provide arbitration schemes, the CIA establishes standards for the education and training of practitioners.

About 50 consumer arbitration schemes have been in operation since the mid-1970s but some parts of the retail and service sector remained outside the process and could only be challenged in the courts. A new Consumer Dispute Resolution Scheme offers a uniform core scheme to assist members of the public who have difficulty in securing resolution of a dispute with a supplier or with the supplier's trade or professional association. The rules of the scheme cover two possible stages, *conciliation* and *arbitration,* conducted by independent conciliators and arbitrators appointed by the Institute. Conciliation will be attempted first unless one or both parties opt to go directly to arbitration. If parties do not settle by conciliation within six weeks, then the dispute will automatically go to arbitration which will result in a binding award within a further 14 weeks.

The advantages of arbitration to the consumer are summarised by the CIA as the independence of the arbitrator, speed, simplicity, certainty and economy (as it is virtually free to the consumer and the supplier cannot seek to recover costs from the complainant), and finality (as the arbitrator's award is legally binding and there is no appeal).

> The scheme is expected to be widely adopted. It will represent tangible evidence of a firm's commitment to its customers in that any dispute which might arise will be resolved speedily, fairly and at minimum cost to the consumer. It will not represent the 'rough justice' currently being advocated in certain quarters but instead a system which complies with the rules of natural justice and which is judged by an arbitrator normally with wide experience of the subject matter of the dispute. Public acceptance of arbitration could lead to substantial savings on the legal aid fund and it is hoped that the national economy will benefit by reducing some of the lengthy, expensive, inequitable and outdated dispute resolution procedures which exist at present.

In 1995, the CIA registered over 2,600 cases for its arbitration scheme, 72 per cent of which concerned disputes between holiday makers and travel companies.

Other processes

The CIA also provides other alternative dispute resolution strategies, including a Conciliation and Mediation Service to 'attempt to reconcile disputants through the good offices of an independent and impartial person' and a Supervised Settlement Procedure, or 'Mini-trial'. In this discussion the focus is on the benefits to the individual in dispute with a corporation; arbitration services are also available for inter-business disputes which fall within *Chapter 11.*

An example of the court system piloting a mediation scheme comes from the Central London County Court. A mediation service for people with disputes involving sums of money over £3,000 is being offered as a quicker, cheaper and less formal alternative to going to court. The process involves a face-to-face meeting plus shuttle diplomacy by the mediator:

> The mediator will be looking for solutions to problems and will be interested in what each side needs as well as what their rights may be. By moving between both sides, carrying information, suggestions, ideas, explanations or offers, the mediator will seek to help everyone to reach a solution to their dispute.

By 1996, the pilot scheme had mediated 47 cases with a further dozen or so in the pipeline. The offer is taken up by a mixture of litigants, both individuals against companies and companies against each other. As discussed in *Chapter 11*, the scheme is benefiting from favourable publicity and an increasing number of enquiries are coming in from solicitors on behalf of clients.

Ombudsmen

A number of ombudsman schemes exist in the UK to investigate individuals' complaints both against public authorities such as local government and the National Health Service or certain private sector services such as insurance and banking. The institution of the ombudsman was created in 1809 in Sweden where it had the task of prosecuting administrators and judges who failed to comply with the law. Ombudsmen were unique to Sweden until 1919, when Finland created a parliamentary ombudsman. More recently, the idea spread to other Scandinavian countries, Denmark in 1955 and Norway in 1963, and in 1962 the first ombudsman scheme in a non-Scandinavian country was set up in New Zealand. World-wide interest followed and by 1995 there were ombudsmen in 75 countries, 27 of them in Europe, including ten in member countries of the European Union. Their establishment reflected the growing awareness on the part of governments about public disquiet at the growth of the power of the state and the consequent perceived powerlessness of the individual to challenge maladministration and unfair treatment. They are seen as a useful way to respond to pressure from organizations campaigning for greater rights, for citizens facing the growing bureaucracy of the state and for greater protection for consumers in an increasingly complex market-place.

Ombudsmen in the public sector

The first ombudsmen in the UK were set up by government in the public sector:

- the Parliamentary Commissioner for Administration in 1967
- the Health Service Ombudsman in 1973 (who is the same person as the Parliamentary Commissioner)
- the five Local Government Ombudsmen in 1974 (three for England and one each for Scotland and Wales).

The Police Complaints Authority, established in 1984, is in effect a public service ombudsman with a highly specialised remit. The terms of reference and powers of the public sector ombudsmen vary but their overall aims and purposes are similar: to provide an alternative dispute resolution mechanism for investigating complaints by private citizens about maladministration, that is about unfair, incompetent, slow or neglectful treatment of the individual by the authority concerned. They are impartial and neutral, have wide powers of investigation and access to documents and can review both the facts of a case and the way in which a decision can be reached. Ombudsmen do not take up individual complaints regarding policy, but focus on those concerning how policy is implemented.

In September 1995, the first Ombudsman of the European Union took up his duties, following models set by national ombudsmen. In his first report, he describes his mission:

> The first and most vital task of the European Ombudsman is to deal with specific instances of maladministration. He must provide an effective means of redress for citizens who are denied their legal rights or who do not receive proper administrative treatment by Community institutions or bodies.
>
> The ombudsman should also help secure the position of citizens by promoting good administrative practices. This involves co-operation with administrative authorities to seek solutions that will improve their relations with citizens.
>
> The Ombudsman also helps to relieve the burdens of litigation, by promoting friendly settlements and by making recommendations that avoid the need for proceedings in court.

The European Ombudsman can only consider complaints about the activities of Community institutions and—up to the end of 1996—80 per cent of the complaints brought to him concerned alleged instances of maladministration by national authorities which are outside his remit. Nearly half of the 83 admissible complaints under consideration came from the UK, a reflection, it could be suggested, of the relatively high profile of public sector ombudsmen within the British system.

Ombudsmen in the private sector

In the 1980s, the idea of ombudsmen spread vigorously into the private sector. The various branches of the financial services industry in particular have set up schemes to facilitate the handling of complaints and the resolution of disputes without resorting to litigation, eg the Insurance Ombudsman Bureau (1981) and the Banking Ombudsman (1986). Other services such as Housing Associations, Estate Agents and Funeral Directors have followed; a list of current schemes is given at the end of the chapter.

Some private sector ombudsmen were set up by legislation, for example the Building Societies and Pensions Ombudsmen; some are voluntary, set up by companies in the industry, such as the Insurance Ombudsman Bureau. Their jurisdictions vary as do their powers. Some can make decisions which are binding, or binding up to a certain monetary level, while some can only make recommendations. Each ombudsman service has its own rules about the scope of cases it will admit and its own procedures for dealing with disputes, though they generally require that complainants exhaust all complaint procedures of the company concerned before coming to the ombudsman. Their offices vary greatly in size, depending on the demand for the service. In a large service such as the Insurance Ombudsman Bureau, the majority of complaints are dealt with by case handling officers investigating the facts and negotiating a settlement. If a complaint cannot be settled by consent and an ombudsman's decision is required, then the case will go to the Ombudsman in person. For example, in 1994 case handlers in the Insurance Ombudsman Bureau resolved 74 per cent of cases using indirect mediation between policyholders and member companies and 26 per cent were referred to the ombudsman for adjudication. The case handler or the ombudsman may decide to bring the parties together at an informal fact-finding hearing but in most cases it is possible to rely solely on paperwork. There is no appeal against a decision for the complainant but if he or she is not satisfied, his or her legal rights to proceed to action in the courts are unaffected.

An example in detail
The Housing Association Ombudsman established in 1993 is small compared with some of the financial services ombudsman schemes. Using four detailed research reports about its work and its Annual Report, a number of issues concerning ombudsman schemes in general can be illustrated, though it should be stressed again that each ombudsman scheme has its own rules and procedures.

The Housing Association Tenants' Ombudsman Service (HATOS) was established in the context of Citizens' Charters whose purpose is to improve the quality of public services and enable and encourage citizens to take action where service does not reach publicised standards. HATOS became operational in November 1993 with objectives:

(a) To provide an accessible, fair and effective means of resolving complaints rightfully made to the ombudsman against registered housing associations by people receiving direct service from them;

(b) To seek redress for complaints, where justified; and

(c) To identify deficiencies in service delivery and help improve the quality of service provided by registered housing associations.

Public consultation prior to the establishment of the service had emphasised that the ombudsman must be independent, powerful and accessible but initially, in order to put the service quickly in place, HATOS was established within the Housing Corporation. After three and a half years, from April 1997, the service will become, by legislation, the Independent Housing Ombudsman Scheme, financed by subscription of participating social landlords. In the Annual Report, the Ombudsman explains:

> 'Social landlords', as defined in the legislation, will be obliged to become members. As well as registered housing associations, a wider group of landlords falls within that definition—including housing companies. The scheme also offers an opportunity for other landlords to join it voluntarily. I hope that this opportunity will be taken up, to secure for more tenants and landlords a way of resolving complaints and disputes.

Independent research showed that tenants found complaints procedures of their housing association difficult to access and slow and unsatisfactory in reaching settlement. The researchers found that many tenants were not informed by their associations that they could appeal to HATOS and recommended efforts to improve publicity and accessibility.

Working practices within HATOS have developed in response to experience. For example, a code of confidentiality has been included in publicity material. Procedures for dealing with complaints have been streamlined and a decision about suitable processes for dealing with each complaint is made as quickly as possible to cut down delays in response. Complaints may be ruled outside the ombudsman's jurisdiction or referred back for completion of local complaints procedures between complainant and housing association. Those to be resolved by the ombudsman are offered a variety of interventions, as the report on setting up the service outlined:

> Uniquely amongst UK Ombudsman schemes, HATOS's formal remit makes provision for resort to mediation and arbitration as well as investigation. Although other Ombudsmen use informal conciliatory methods, HATOS alone has contracted a professional mediation service to be used in the resolution of disputes where such informal approaches have failed or are inappropriate. Mediation involves enabling both sides of a dispute to assess and come to terms with their situation before formulating

and agreeing a solution. The provision of 'mediation' or conciliation to resolve complaints was an integral part of the setting up of HATOS and was included in the public consultation document.

HATOS has contracted IDR Europe Limited to be its outside professional mediation service, and also proposed to co-operate with mediation schemes under the auspices of Mediation UK in order to appoint suitable mediators for each case. Although the ombudsman could himself or herself act as arbitrator in those cases where arbitration is suitable, in practice an independent arbitrator is appointed by the Chartered Institute of Arbitrators. In his Annual Report for 1995-6, the ombudsman was able to state that:

> We have made increasing use of alternative dispute resolution. Its availability seems to be better known, and we have often suggested it to parties earlier in our consideration of their cases.
>
> During the year over 50 cases have been referred to mediation. Of the mediation cases completed in the year, 22 resulted in a successful agreement between parties; four were not successful; and five were withdrawn for various reasons. A few cases have successfully been resolved through arbitration. Additionally in a few cases I have made informal adjudications by agreement with the parties. I believe all these approaches to dispute resolution are an integral part of my function.

In practice mediation has not been used as much as had been expected. Feedback from tenants' associations showed that more awareness raising and information is required for full appreciation of the benefits of the process.

An example of a case from the Annual Report illustrates how similar some of the mediation work of HATOS is to the work of community mediation services.

> The complainant's tenancy agreement said that the garage at the rear of two properties owned by the association was to be shared for storage purposes but cars should not be kept there. The complainant had fallen out with the adjoining tenant. As a result, she had been denied use of the shared garage and of the gate at the rear of her property. The association had tried to provide suitable alternative storage facilities for the complainant which she had not accepted. During mediation, the association immediately restored the complainant's rights to the garage and to her use of the gateway. I understand that the dispute between the tenants themselves has gone to separate mediation organized locally by the association.

A second example illustrates how a group of tenants can benefit from the mediation process, but again this dispute could have equally been mediated by a local community mediation service working with the housing association and the tenants' group:

> The complainant came to me on his own behalf and also as chairman of a residents association complaining about the poor management by the association of two groups of properties. I received clear details of the disputes. The parties readily accepted that they should try to resolve matters through mediation. A first mediation meeting resulted in an interim agreement. Two months later a second meeting developed the areas of agreement. In particular the mediation agreement dealt with future communication and the meeting arrangements between the association and the residents association. The mediation also settled the agenda for a subsequent meeting between the residents association and the housing association to deal with particular matters regarding the management of the estates.

The research demonstrated that satisfaction rates of users are high. Just under two thirds of the sample of complainants found complaining to the ombudsman worthwhile, whether their complaint had been taken up or not. Many of those who were referred back to their housing association reported that they had received rapid satisfaction once it was known that they had approached the ombudsman. Ninety-six per cent of the sample of associations responding to the research reported satisfaction at the way HATOS has dealt with complaints.

Another interesting research finding was that a disproportionate number of complaints came from people aged over 60, probably because people of this age group are likely to spend more time at home and be more affected by any problems arising from their accommodation. The research comments that this merits further investigation and collaboration with EMP (see page 39) would seem to be a way forward. Overall the research concluded that HATOS has been of great value to tenants. It recommended that monitoring of complainants' expectations and experiences should continue, including the long term outcomes of mediation, and that increased publicity, information and advice should be offered to enable more tenants to take advantage of the scheme.

Advantages and disadvantages of using ombudsmen schemes

Ombudsman services are free, confidential, and thorough. They aim to be user friendly and most publicity material supplied by respondents is clear and helpful in explaining the sorts of cases that they will deal with. They are able to award a satisfactory settlement to the disputant without the stress, time and expense of taking a case to court. Usually, the disputant retains his or her legal rights to pursue the claim in law if it is not upheld by an ombudsman and so has nothing to lose.

Once complaints pass the initial screening, the success rate at some services is high; for example, 90 per cent of outcomes of cases investigated by the Parliamentary Ombudsman in 1992 were either wholly or partly in favour of the complainant. This contrasts with, for example, a 35 per cent success rate for complainants to the Insurance Ombudsman Bureau and 53 per cent of cases found in favour of the complainant by the Banking Ombudsman in 1995.

The disadvantages of taking a complaint to an ombudsman service are that a dispute may fall outside the relevant ombudsman's jurisdiction and not be investigated at all. For example, in 1992 the Parliamentary Ombudsman only received 945 complaints (from a population of 55 million people), of which he accepted 269 for investigation. In 1995-6, the Local Government Ombudsman for Scotland received 1,028 complaints of which 814 were not accepted for formal investigation. Another disadvantage for the individual is that the outcome of a case is hard to predict and because the details of cases are confidential a disputant cannot know how the outcome of his case compares to that in other cases. Further, as the powers of ombudsmen are limited, the size of the settlement can only reflect what they are empowered to recommend. They may also have difficulty in gaining access to all the documents required for their investigations; for example, the European Ombudsman is calling for guaranteed right of access to all official documents to ensure that the principles of openness and transparency are put into practice.

Generally low awareness of the function and services of ombudsmen can be attributed to their relatively recent arrival as an alternative means of resolving disputes; it also means that reasons for low take-up by the public need to be examined and addressed.

Regulators

Consumer complaints in newly privatised service industries—telephone services, rail services, water, gas and electricity supply—are part of a government appointed watchdog system of regulators. Regulators have wide powers to influence the way the industries operate, but consumer protection is also an important aspect of their work. Each industry has set up its own system for consumer protection; for example OFTEL (the telephone regulator) has responsibility both for economic regulation of the industry and for consumer protection whereas in the gas industry OFGAS is responsible for economic regulation and the Gas Consumers' Councils deal with consumer complaints.

The complaints procedures set up by regulators take up cases which a company supplying a service fails to resolve by internal procedures. Recommendations and decisions are made after investigation but unlike ombudsman schemes there is no ultimate decision maker or power to make a final decision.

Wider powers of ombudsmen and regulators

Some ombudsmen and regulators also have an advocacy and monitoring role. Ombudsmen may make recommendations about the conduct of organizations in their sector and recommend improvements in procedures. For example, in his eighth Annual Report, the Banking Ombudsman called on banks to improve their codes of good practice by giving more information to explain their recommendation of particular products, so that customers are able to make a more informed decision between, for example, an endowment or a repayment mortgage. He also suggested that fuller statements should be given by banks to their customers about how charges and interest payments are calculated. Regulators have powers to limit price rises and even to cut prices of services and products in the privatised utilities. These additional functions are aimed at creating public satisfaction and a sense of fairness and are part of the role that ombudsmen and regulators play in representing the interests of David against Goliath.

CONCLUSION

This chapter has reviewed some mechanisms that have been developed to investigate citizens' complaints and redress justifiable grievances. The growth in power and bureaucracy of public authorities and private corporations has emphasised the powerlessness of the individual and created public pressure for new forms of accountability to safeguard the rights of ordinary people. Alternatives to the traditional justice system offer cheaper, swifter and fairer ways for citizens and consumers to pursue their complaints and grievances. The detailed case study of an ombudsman scheme illustrates the potential for the development of a variety of ADR strategies within such a service. It also indicates that collaboration between an ombudsman schemes and other mediation and ADR services can be fruitful.

Questions arise concerning the accessibility of these processes. Are they sufficiently and clearly enough publicised so that people generally know of their existence and feel able to use them? Are they effective enough in redressing the balance of power between the individual and the public authority or private corporation? In what ways should their powers be strengthened and extended? How can access to all documents required for an investigation be guaranteed? Are adequate remedies available when fault has been proved? Can a private sector ombudsman credibly maintain his or her independence from the industry that funds his or her work? Although David has his chance against Goliath, in the real world is the power still with the big battalions? (Although David later became the King of Israel and a role model for medieval princes, it does not follow that people who gain redress from ombudsmen will become state leaders!)

Ombudsmen and regulators

The list of Ombudsmen and Regulators is summarised from the Lord Chancellor's Department publication *Resolving Disputes Without Going to Court*. Numbers of complaints received by Ombudsmen for 1993 are quoted from *Social Trends 1995* in which it is noted that 'each organization has its own systems of recording complaints or cases and some are affected by certain legislation so the figures are not strictly comparable. Some figures include complaints or cases from the previous year, some include cases which are later found to be outside the terms of reference of the office. Also, the reporting year varies; some are based on the financial year while others use calendar years. With these caveats, the figures give a picture of the level of complaints brought to the ombudsmen services.

Public Sector

Parliamentary Ombudsman	986
Health Service Ombudsman	1,384
Local Government Ombudsman	16,507
Northern Ireland Ombudsman	605
Police Complaints Authority	17,991
Police Complaints (Northern Ireland)	2,419

Private Sector

Legal Services Ombudsman	1,235
Banking Ombudsman	10,231
Broadcasting Complaints Ombudsman	1,049
Building Societies Ombudsman	9,142
Corporate Estate Agents Ombudsman[2]	2,340
Funeral Ombudsman	(figure not supplied)
Insurance Ombudsman	8,133
Investment Ombudsman	103
Pensions Ombudsman	2,179
Personal Investment Authority Ombudsman	(established 1995)
Housing Association Tenants Ombudsman	1,040
Prisons Ombudsman	(figure not supplied).

---

[2] Since 1 January 1998, Ombudsman for Estate Agents

Regulators
Office of Water Services (OFWAT)
Office of Gas Supply (OFGAS)
Office of Electricity Regulation (OFFER)
Office of Telecommunications (OFTEL)
Office of Passenger Rail Franchising (OPFRA)

SOURCES AND FURTHER READING: *Chapter 10*

Annual Reports and Publications of Chartered Institute of Arbitrators and each Ombudsman and Regulator

Birkenshaw, P., *Grievances, Remedies and the State,* 1995 edition

Central London County Court, *Mediation Pilot Scheme,* 1996

European Voice

Graham, C., *The Non-Classical Ombudsman,* University of Sheffield, 1991.

Housing Association Tenants Ombudsman Service, *Research Reports 1-4* and *Annual Report 1995-6*

Official Journal of the European Communities

'Ombudsman Calls on Banks to Improve', *The Guardian,* 7 December 1996

Lord Chancellor's Department, *Resolving Disputes Without Going to Court,* HMSO

Seneviratne, M., *Ombudsmen in the Public Sector,* 1994

Social Trends, 25, 26 and 27, 1995, 1996 and 1997

Veljanovski, C., (Ed.) *Regulators and the Market: An Assessment of the Growth of Regulation in the UK,* 1991.

Acknowledgments
Chartered Instititute of Arbitrators
Central London County Court
Insurance Ombudsman Service
Housing Association Tenants' Ombudsman Service.

CHAPTER 11

The World of Work

Oh my friends, the down-trodden operatives of Coketown! Oh my friends and fellow countrymen, the slaves of an iron-handed and a grinding despotism! Oh my friends and fellow sufferers and fellow workmen, and fellow men! I tell you that the hour is come when we must rally round one another as One united power, and crumble into dust the oppressors that too long have battened upon the plunder of our families, upon the sweat of our brows, upon the labour of our hands, upon the strength of our sinews, upon the God-created glorious rights of Humanity and upon the holy and eternal privileges of Brotherhood.

Hard Times: Charles Dickens

The mission of the Advisory, Conciliation and Arbitration Service (ACAS) is to improve the performance and effectiveness of organizations by providing an independent and impartial service to prevent and resolve disputes and to build harmony at work.

ACAS Annual Report

The literature of industrial relations abounds in the discourse of conflict. The history of the trade union movement recounts many episodes of violence and bitter confrontation between workers and bosses. The feelings expressed by Slackbridge, the union delegate in Coketown in 1854, just three years after the foundation of the Amalgamated Engineering Union, the first modern style union, were not so different from those voiced in the miners' strike in 1984-5. If any area of activity can benefit from alternative dispute strategies, it must be the field of industrial relations.

This chapter reviews various aspects of conflict resolution in the world of work. The questionnaire responses (*Chapter 3*) are reviewed and ADR strategies used to manage collective disputes between management and workforce are outlined, as well as the mechanisms for resolving the workplace disputes of individuals. Discussion then focuses on the development of conflict resolution services for companies who are in dispute with each other.

PATTERNS OF ADR

Twenty-one respondents indicated that they were active in the field of industrial or commercial mediation:

• trade unions	8
• public agencies, eg courts and statutory bodies	3
• voluntary and private services eg consultancy, solicitors, mediation services	10

Table 11.1: Respondents Involved in Industrial or Commercial Mediation

Thirty-three respondents indicated that they were involved in negotiation/conciliation services, 13 of them also being active in industrial or commercial mediation. Negotiation/conciliation services were an activity of a wide range of organizations, on offer internally to staff in dispute or to member organizations and individuals:

• trade unions	9
• public agencies	2
• private services	6
• social services	3
• education	1
• police	3
• CVS and other voluntary organizations	6
• housing association/tenants advice	2
• probation	1

Table 11.2: Organizations With Negotiation/Conciliation Services

The trade unions and professional associations which responded gave details of their work as negotiators on behalf of their workers. One of the largest unions, under the heading 'Winning for members' claims:

We have a first-class record of winning for our members. We have successfully negotiated over pay and conditions time and time again. You can be certain that our experienced officers will understand and deal with any problems you may have. Your union representatives are there to help you improve conditions in the workplace. We regularly successfully defend workers who have been unfairly dismissed from work. We are working toward the elimination of discrimination at work and will support and represent members at Industrial Tribunals in cases of equal pay for work of equal value and discrimination on the grounds of race or colour.

The objectives of another union with a membership of 250,000 are stated in less confrontational terms:

The main objectives of the union are to protect and promote the interests of members and improve their working lives. As an industry-wide union, we are committed to achieving the highest possible membership levels, as the union feels that this is the best way to protect individual employees, improve general working conditions and increase the influence of the Union, both with employers and other bodies such as the Government, industry regulators and the European Commission.

COLLECTIVE BARGAINING

The first responsibility of trade unions is to promote the interests of their members and as such they are advocates rather than peacemakers. However, often the interests of members are best served by the resolution or prevention of conflict by negotiation. By uniting into a union, the negotiating or bargaining position of the individual member becomes collectively strengthened so that the imbalance in power between workers and employer is reduced. There are many texts which give an account of the history of the trade union movement and describe current law relating to employment which forms the framework of labour relations. From these, it is possible to trace the rise in power and influence of unions from the mid-nineteenth century to their heyday in the post-1945 period, followed by the radical curtailment of their powers by legislation during the 1980s and early 1990s. From a high point of 53 per cent in 1980 in 1994, 32 per cent of the workforce in employment were trade union members; though this is still 8.3 million individuals. At the end of 1994 there were 243 unions in the UK of which seven accounted for 59 per cent of the membership.

The attack on trade union powers in the 1980s was part of government policy to deregulate and dismantle any institution or practice which hindered the free operation of the marketplace. Collective bargaining, the traditional machinery developed by trade unions to institutionalise the struggle to improve the terms and conditions of employment of their members, came under attack as a practice restricting the free operation of the labour market. At the same time as new management strategies both in the private and public sectors encourage local pay bargaining and individual performance packages, recession and high unemployment further weakened both the membership and influence of unions. Manufacturing industry, the stronghold of unionism, has been critically eroded and workers in low paid service industries feel insecure and isolated. Because the balance of power between unions and employers has shifted markedly in favour of employers, the skills of trade union negotiators in using alternative dispute resolution procedures are crucially exercised to preserve and maximise such bargaining opportunities as remain.

Negotiation is the process whereby collective bargaining takes place. Negotiators representing the two sides, management and workers, set their objectives and tactically manoeuvre to achieve a settlement. Each side sets an ideal target, a realistic outcome and a fallback position beyond which it will not go. If the two sides are well prepared, it is likely that their target positions will overlap and that the settlement will fall within the overlapping area. Each side will have compromised and moved from its ideal target but each side will feel it has won some ground. At each stage, propositions or offers are supported by arguments to demonstrate the strength of commitment to the proposition. Adjustment on each part of the settlement will bring the sides closer to an overall agreement.

Failure to reach agreement will trigger a dispute procedure which may use third party intervention by conciliators, mediators or arbitrators provided by the Advisory Conciliation and Arbitration Service (ACAS).

An example of union practice

The public service union UNISON is the largest union in the UK, formed in 1993 by the amalgamation of the National Association of Local Government Officers, the National Union of Public Employees and the Health Service Employees union. Its membership is thus spread between local government, the health services and a wide range of public services some of which are now contracted out to private agencies. UNISON is organized into 13 regions.

UNISON sees itself primarily as an advocate for its members, working on their behalf to achieve the best possible pay and conditions of service from their employers. In doing this, it is involved in conflict resolution, but this would not generally be perceived as an objective. A slow change in the culture of the union is coming about in response to the change in membership from predominantly full-time male workers in a job for life to a mixture of full-time and part-time, male and female, workers, many of them on flexible contracts. In the old culture, the union bosses were male, confrontational, eager to fight cases and win. They tended to take disputes immediately out of the control of the individual or group experiencing the problem, to have their day in the industrial tribunal sparring with the employer. This confrontational strategy is gradually giving way to a more 'female' approach of search for compromise in informal discussion, using local procedures in a more collaborative, problem-solving way.

Now that there is a balance between local and national bargaining, with a range from all pay and conditions negotiated locally to national bargaining and branches negotiating around national framework agreements, many more negotiators at local level need to be trained in skills to negotiate the local implementation of agreements. This offers opportunities for openness and fairness and more participation in debate by members. Issues such as voluntary redundancy packages, equal opportunities and health and safety concerns are negotiated locally, all of which involve a new style of negotiation aimed at conflict prevention. Workplace bargaining gives UNISON members more control of different aspects of their work situations as is described in a *Guide on Local Bargaining:*

> There should never be a shortage of issues to take up with management. The problem should be prioritising them.
>
> Where pay is bargained locally, the pay round is the most obvious opportunity for advancing the pay and conditions of the workforce — but it does not mean that the union should go into hibernation for the rest of the year. The union will be kept busy with proposals from employers to make changes or reorganize, including job evaluation, and regrading exercises. And there will be opportunities to take up issues on behalf of members, such as, health and safety, grading appeals, improved maternity and paternity pay and leave, carer's leave. In fact, negotiations are often more likely to occur on these issues than pay on its own.

The guide gives plentiful details on how to conduct negotiations on pay and conditions, including tactics in negotiations and strategies to use in meetings, such as advice on having one person in the team as spokesperson, note-taking and adjournments for consultation.

> Negotiations are a process of exchange, of ongoing dialogue between the employers and the members. It is important to keep that exchange going, if there are to be serious negotiations, and progress is to be made towards achieving the union's goals. It benefits both union members and employers that negotiations are carried out efficiently and for an acceptable agreement to be reached. There will always be need for compromise by both sides and, although negotiations may become difficult, the framework for a possible final deal needs to be kept in mind.

While stressing the need for union strength, there is also room for mutual problem solving:

> Some experienced negotiators like to view the process of negotiation as being an exercise in mutual problem solving. Thus agreeing on a pay and conditions claim is viewed as a 'problem' which the two sides are jointly attempting to solve. This approach bases itself on identifying as much common ground as possible between the two sides. It has the merit of depersonalising negotiations; identifying the possibility of making progress on the basis of common ground; stops each side tying itself into

135

antagonistic positions; and looks to the interests of the parties rather than their positions.

These extracts demonstrate clearly the conflict resolution role of the union.

Local shop stewards have a role in supporting their members in disputes with management and are trained to look for a workable resolution of a conflict by negotiating on a give-and-take basis. If the dispute is too serious for the shop steward to handle, then he or she will go for assistance to a full-time union case handler. The East Midlands Region of UNISON alone has about 40 full-time case handlers who between them at any time will be dealing with up to 2,000 disputes. The majority of disputes centre on workers' fears of dismissal where employers are using sickness records or job performance indicators to establish grounds for ending or not renewing contracts of employment. Some disputes are between individual and employer; in others, often in a newly privatised agency, groups of workers are experiencing the fear of losing their jobs. Union case handlers will try to use the employer's internal procedures to resolve disputes but negotiations may reach a status of 'failure to agree'. The UNISON Guide gives details of the next step in a disputes procedure. The options are likely to be:

> Further negotiations, perhaps involving full-time officers and more senior management;
> Conciliation, mediation or arbitration involving a third party;
> Sanctions—such as industrial action by the workforce, or a lockout by the employer, or unilateral changes to terms and conditions by the employer.

It explains that a mediator takes an active role in suggesting ways in which a dispute might be solved while a conciliator helps to clarify issues and liaises between the parties but does not offer solutions. If there is no dispute procedure or a complete failure to agree by any of the suggested strategies, the union will usually support calling on the services of ACAS before considering sanctions as a last resort.

ACAS

ACAS, the Advisory, Conciliation and Arbitration Service was established in 1974 as an independent service funded by central government to provide conciliation, mediation and arbitration facilities for dealing with collective and individual disputes between employers and employees. Its publicity stresses the accessibility of its services to individuals, unions and employers through its 12 regional offices. It also has general functions to provide information and advice and to promote good practice in employment and industrial relations.

ACAS offers the services of a conciliator as a first resort when collective bargaining between parties has failed to reach a settlement. The aim is to bring the parties together quickly to clarify differences and sort out misunderstandings so that a swift settlement can be achieved and escalation of the dispute avoided. The conciliator has no powers to make recommendations but acts as a facilitator and go-between, leaving the parties always in control of their own bargaining positions. Such disputes are generally those defined in the Industrial Relations Act 1971 as disputes of right which relate to the application or interpretation of existing agreements or contracts of employment.

Where disputes arise from underlying difficulties and need long-term solutions, ACAS provides the services of an advisory mediator who will engage more actively than a conciliator in suggesting possible solutions. Mediation assists in disputes arising from organizational change involving alterations in working practices; these are defined as 'disputes of interest, which relate to claims by employees or proposals by management about terms and conditions of employment.'

The parties may fail to reach a settlement, or be unwilling to engage in advisory mediation, and instead move straight to arbitration. The ACAS arbitrator will decide the issue on the basis of the cases presented by the parties who will agree to be bound by the decision. It is generally understood that the arbitrator will decide within the range of options and outcomes tabled by the two parties. In the 1980s *pendulum* or *final offer* arbitration, used in the USA since the 1930s, was adopted in some agreements in the UK. This required the arbitrator to decide on the final position of one or other of the parties rather than to 'split the difference'. It encourages another American practice, mediation arbitration (known as *med-arb*), where the mediator works to narrow the gap between the parties and recommends the final positions to the arbitrator for decision. The disadvantages of pendulum arbitration for the future working relationship of the parties are that it produces a clear win/lose result and can often include a no-strike clause, unpopular from the union point of view.

The process of negotiation continues through all the stages of collective bargaining and dispute procedures. If at any stage before arbitration negotiations critically break down and the dispute moves to confrontational industrial action, ACAS continues to work to bring the two sides back to the negotiating table. Legislation in the 1980s introduced complex compulsory balloting procedures before industrial action could lawfully begin, as well as restrictions on picketing and increased powers for employers to dismiss strikers, obtain injunctions preventing industrial action and sue unions for non-compliance. As a result, the number of official work stoppages fell from over 1,000 a year in the early 1980s to a little over 200 a year in the early 1990s. In 1993 the 211 stoppages were fewer than in any year since records began in 1891. From a peak of nearly 30 million working days lost in the year of the Winter of Discontent (1979), only 415,000 working days were lost as a result of labour disputes in 1995. This dramatic fall, however, is principally a result of government policy, legislation, the effects of recession and the decline of manufacturing industry and consequent deep changes in the culture of industrial relations rather the success of alternative dispute resolution strategies.

INDIVIDUAL DISPUTES IN THE WORKPLACE

The UNISON guide explains that the services of ACAS are available to individuals in dispute with their employers. The law in the UK requires that employees receive a written statement of their main terms and conditions of employment and this will specify disciplinary and grievance procedures to be followed if either side is dissatisfied with the behaviour or performance of the other. Where employees are members of a union recognised by the employers, union representatives will act for or alongside employees in dispute and representatives of both management and union are likely to be involved in deciding the outcome of disputes. If they fail to agree, or an individual is advised by his or her union to appeal against the decision to an industrial tribunal, then ACAS has a statutory duty to offer its services to try to bring about a settlement. The number of individual cases received by ACAS covering unfair dismissal, equal pay, sex or race discrimination has been growing since the mid-1980s to nearly 80,000 in 1994. Thirty-one per cent of cases were withdrawn after informal discussions to be settled internally; in 37 per cent of cases ACAS conciliators achieved an agreed settlement; 32 per cent proceeded to arbitration before a tribunal.

INTERNAL PROCEDURES

Many organizations counter that negotiation and conciliation services are part of their activity in the sense of work within their internal staff development programmes. They also have in mind the work of negotiation and conciliation performed as part of management functions in particular in association with internal disciplinary and grievance procedures. For example, the resolution of a sexual harassment dispute between members of staff is the responsibility of the employer. Before proceeding to disciplinary action, management must investigate the allegation to see if there is a case to be answered. If the victim of harassment is a union member, support will be given by their union representative who will be looking for a management solution which will separate the parties and perhaps oblige the harasser to attend training for behaviour change.

The increased use of ADR in different situations has raised awareness in workplaces that disciplinary and grievance procedures, far from settling disputes, polarise feelings and encourage destructive adversarial confrontation between the parties involved. There is anecdotal evidence that some managers are beginning to consider using mediation strategies before or alongside disciplinary or grievance procedures. For example, a community mediation service in the West Midlands has been called in to a large local organization to mediate in a dispute between two employees as an alternative to the formal grievance procedure which was driving them deeper into conflict. In another Midlands organization, managers have offered independent mediation between a head of department and staff if both sides will agree to participate as part of the resolution of a complex interpersonal dispute.

A further example of similar development resulted from a wide-ranging research programme undertaken by a northern police force into its policies and practices regarding equal opportunities and racial and sexual harassment. One result of the findings has been the development of a care scheme to support staff who are feeling isolated, rejected or discriminated against by the behaviour of others. An aggrieved person can make first contact with an adviser whose role is to provide confidential support, to be a listening ear, with whom the range of options open to the complainant can be discussed and if necessary the adviser may act as a go-between. This scheme is an example of conflict prevention, providing an informal mechanism for dealing with grievances which may prevent the development of a formally constituted dispute.

VOLUNTARY SECTOR INITIATIVES

In the voluntary sector, the umbrella Councils of Voluntary Service are increasingly being called upon to take on the role of mediation in disputes involving their members. In recognition of this, the National Council for Voluntary Organizations (NCVO) is setting up a new service 'to offer an effective intervention in the kinds of internal dispute that sometimes threaten to undermine the enthusiasm and commitment and hard work of charities and voluntary organizations.' They will ask a mediator from a panel of experienced mediation practitioners to work with the parties in dispute to 'identify common ground for alleviating both the distress being caused to individuals and the damage to the work of the organization itself.' The experience of the NCVO suggests that disputes among trustees, between trustees and staff, among staff and between branches of national charities and their central organizations could all benefit from such a mediation service.

COMMERCIAL ADR SERVICES

Independent commercial mediation and ADR services are a growing field. The ADR Group founded in 1989 and the Centre for Dispute Resolution (CEDR) launched in 1990 are currently among the leading private commercial dispute resolution services in the UK. The ADR Group was established by lawyers, business and professional mediators to provide a quick and inexpensive service for disputants without the need to resort to the courts. The company administers cases referred by insurance companies, solicitors, accountants and industry. It has a pool of over 120 trained legal mediators, known as the ADR Net, who subscribe to the solicitors' code of conduct. CEDR is a non-profit making organization which uses the subscriptions and commitment of its 300 plus members to promote ADR in legal, business and public sector practice. It claims 'to be the flagship for raising understanding, profile and use of ADR procedures such as mediation across the full spectrum of disputes'. Typically a commercial mediation is a short and intense process, often a single day during which the parties get together in the same building and sometimes in the same room with the mediator acting as a go-between to assist them in finding and agreeing a settlement.

Commercial disputes do not stay within national boundaries and mediation services are working with trading partners in Europe and the global market. The London Court of International Arbitration is an example of an organization which provides services for international commercial arbitration. When parties making arbitration agreements through its services require conciliation or mediation services, they are referred on to CEDR which has a growing number of overseas clients. The European Union is concerned with providing a framework for resolving disputes between commercial organizations in different member states or disputes which involve the interests of individuals in more than one country of the Union. For example, at a very detailed level, the Conciliation Committee of the European Parliament is currently working to reach agreement on the exact terms and wording of a Directive on investor-compensation schemes. This process is itself a negotiation between the interests of member states, and between the perspectives of the European Parliament and the Commission, as well as being about the setting up of mechanisms to resolve disputes in a particular commercial area. An example involving both commercial and environmental issues is given in the case study in *Chapter 9*.

The benefits of ADR in commercial settings are being increasingly recognised and new developments discussed and evaluated. For example, the Association of British Insurers produces a regular overview of recent work in ADR for distribution to insurance companies. In recent issues, it has summarised the main provision of the Arbitration Act 1996 which aims to improve and refine current arbitration law, so that businesses and other users of arbitration have access to a speedier, cheaper and fair system of resolving disputes. Information about pilot court based mediation and ADR projects, ADR seminars and conferences and the formation of new independent dispute resolution firms is also included in the report. Articles in the legal press also comment on the latest developments in the field. A recent such article suggested that the low take-up of one of the court-based pilot schemes reflects the cautious attitude of some solicitors to mediation:

> Some practitioners seem to think that mediation adds nothing to competent negotiations between solicitors. However, skilful 'shuttle diplomacy' by experienced mediators can often help the parties find common ground, sometimes by including non-legal elements in the agreement. There is concern that the official approval of mediation by the Lord Chancellor's Department and the courts could be motivated mainly by a desire to reduce the costs of litigation and therefore solicitors' incomes. But there is evidence that many citizens are very reluctant to embark on litigation through fear of costs. There is a clear role for legal advisers in many mediations.[1]

This article encouraged an upsurge of enquiries about the scheme from solicitors. The *Financial Times* in an article in January 1997 expressed the hope of the arbitration community 'that the new system will restore London's reputation as a centre for resolving international disputes'.[2] The article explains the improvements introduced by the new Act in terms of clarity of approach and the greater powers given to arbitrators. An international lawyer is quoted as wondering how arbitrators and parties will respond to radically improved powers. 'Will they have the courage to use them?' The launch by a UK law firm of a unit dedicated to ADR was greeted as a 'significant boost' to 'the acceptance of ADR in the UK as an effective means of resolving commercial disputes'.[3] The

---

[1] *Law Society Gazette* 94, 8 January 1997

[2] *Financial Times*, 28 January 1997

[3] *Financial Times*, 1 July 1997

American lawyer heading the unit declared, 'Whether the English legal profession likes it or not, mediation is here to stay.'

There is clearly an increase in interest and in the use of mediation in the commercial field and an opportunity for specialist enterprise to meet a growing demand from clients. Such enterprise is being shown by the law department at a northern university which is planning to set up an ADR service for local businesses within the ADR Net. Having completed mediation training, they now have to market their service which it is hoped will both generate income for the department and provide a practice ground in mediation skills for their students.

CONCLUSION

The traditional mechanisms of collective bargaining and dispute procedures used to manage industrial relations have institutionalised conflict between employers and employees. Will the decline in the role of trade unions continue in the face of the reassertion of managerial authority? What future has collective representation of employees in the new structures of industrial relations? How successfully will local bargaining develop as a strategy for conflict resolution in the workplace? How far will job insecurity deter workers from engaging in negotiation? How far will mediation as a strategy for resolving interpersonal disputes penetrate into the workplace? All that seems certain is that the pace of change is likely to accelerate.

The use of ADR strategies in commercial disputes has been welcomed for its speed and cost-effectiveness compared with costly court litigation. While some lawyers see the advantage of developing mediation services alongside their legal practice, solicitors generally seem reluctant to recommend alternative solutions to their clients. The discussion has focused on processes and developments in the UK, but the European dimension and the growth of world markets and multi-national companies will increasingly create a need for internationally recognised and practised commercial ADR.

SOURCES AND FURTHER READING: *Chapter 11*

Bevan, A., *Alternative Dispute Resolution: A Lawyer's Guide to Mediation and Other Forms of Dispute Resolution*, 1992
Burchill, F., *Labour Relations*, 1992
'Better Room For Argument', *Financial Times*, 28 January 1997
'Centre for Consensus', *Financial Times*, 1 July 1997

Income Data Services, *Industrial Relations and Collective Bargaining*, Institute of Personnel and Development: European Management Guide, 1996

Law Society Gazette, 8 January 1997

Mackie, K. N. (Ed.), *A Handbook of Dispute Resolution: ADR in Action*, 1991

Millward, N., *The New Industrial Relations?*, Policy Studies Institute 1994,

Social Trends, 1995, 1996 and 1997

UNISON Policy and Research, *Local Bargaining: A Guide for UNISON Negotiators*, 1993.

Acknowledgments

ACAS

UNISON, East Midlands Region

Communications Workers Union

Transport and General Workers Union

London Court of International Arbitration

Association of British Insurers

CEDR

ADR Net

National Council for Voluntary Organizations

University of Hull, Law Department.

CHAPTER 12

Training

The skills you learn as a mediator never leave you. You will be able to use them at home and work. Many people who take this course feel their view of the world and themselves changes permanently for the better.

Cardiff Mediation

It is essential in order that consumers of mediation services may be properly protected, that mediators can be confident of their ability to provide an excellent service, and that [the profession] is not brought into disrepute by practitioners mediating without the necessary skills or understanding of the personal, practical, legal and ethical issues involved.

Solicitors' Family Law Association

The two views expressed about training in mediation skills approach the issue from different perspectives—the learner-centred and the profession-centred. This dichotomy forms one of the undercurrents in a diversity of approaches to training. Other issues to emerge are training for 'what' and by 'whom'—issues of quality, structure and credibility. The need for training is widely recognised and a lot of resources in terms of time and funding are devoted by most organizations to training programmes. Sixty per cent of respondents provide in-house training for their volunteers and staff; 90 per cent take advantage of external training opportunities for a proportion of, or even all, their mediators each year.

Although mediation and alternative dispute resolution share a central core of basic skills, specialised fields demand additional skills. Practitioners of family or victim-offender mediation need areas of knowledge and expertise which are not essential for a neighbourhood mediator. Negotiating skills are needed by all those engaged in conflict resolution, but for those engaged in collective bargaining a special understanding of the procedures is required. Different qualifications are demanded of those who specialise in commercial arbitration.

This chapter examines three main areas of training, ie that of: volunteer mediators; professionals involved in mediation and ADR; and the trainers themselves.

Training volunteer mediators
Assertions such as 'Mediation is about enabling people to resolve their own conflicts. It must not become an area where experts take over' and

'We are a group of ordinary women and men from the area . . .' are almost invariably followed by the information that the mediators are 'trained in mediation skills', and even 'fully trained'. The volunteers who came together to form community mediation groups in the 1980s recognised that they needed training in mediation skills to be able to offer their service confidently to neighbours in dispute. One of the pioneer groups, the Kingston Friends, ran workshops and prepared training materials that many other groups used and found helpful and supportive. In their *Introduction to Mediation*, the Kingston Friends Workshop Group explained their learner-centred approach to mediation training:

> Whilst informal mediation has taken place over countless generations, standardised conflict resolution training is relatively new, still developing and being evaluated. In general, we do not recommend training to be a mediator from a book or workpack alone; skills need to be tried and refined in relation to other people.
>
> Mediation is only one of a range of conflict resolution processes and techniques, but the underlying skills are common to all creative methods of dealing with disputes and difficulties in personal relationships. Specific mediation training is not wasted, if it does not lead to formal mediation; the skills, experience and insights that are gained play an important part in the management of interpersonal relationships and conflicts at many levels.

Mediation UK provides information about training and trainers to its members and sponsors training events for mediators who wish to develop their skills. In the early 1990s a Mediation UK Training Manual Working Party collated best current practice incorporating materials from different groups and information and inspiration from ENCORE and the Quaker Education Advisory Programme to produce in 1996 the first British *Training Manual in Community Mediation Skills*. Together with videos and other materials, this is designed to provide a structured framework with practical resources for mediation training 'which will allow for diversity and choice, enabling trainers, mediators and services to put their own stamp on training courses and mediation practices'. The sections of the manual reflect the process of learning to be a mediator: 'What is Mediation'; 'Getting Ready to Mediate'; 'Working as a Mediator'; 'Evaluation and Assessment'. The manual has been supplemented by a handbook for tutors which lays out a training programme of four 30 hour units of study which are accredited with the Open College Network at levels 2 and 3 (unit 4 at level 3 only). This accredited programme provides a nationally recognised standard of competence for community mediators to which volunteers have access through local training courses. Further, an agreed NVQ standard between all the branches of mediation is awaiting qualifying award development.

Mediation UK has put in place an accreditation scheme which offers formal accredited status for established mediation services which submit on a voluntary basis to external assessment of their systems, processes and quality of service. By the end of 1996 the scheme was still new; four services had been awarded accreditation and many more had either started the process or were thinking about entering the scheme.

The majority of voluntary neighbourhood mediation services who responded that they ran their own in-house training for their volunteers were not, at the time of their response, linked to any accreditation scheme. About half mentioned that they based their training on the Mediation UK Manual (this does not mean that others did not), a quarter mentioned OCN accreditation and a few have developed an NVQ assessment scheme. Most training is not accredited though some groups mentioned that they were looking into the possibilities; one respondent was 'waiting to see whether accreditation of mediation is likely to follow NVQ path or OCN'.

A typical locally produced package involves between 25 and 40 hours of training sessions, usually divided into some all-day workshops and some evening sessions. The sequence and context of the training packages varied slightly, with a balance between understanding conflict and conflict behaviour, learning the skills and practising them in role plays. Most were followed up by either regular meetings of volunteers, occasional workshops, opportunities to attend external training events and, in a few instances, one-to-one supervision sessions with experienced practitioners. Newly trained mediators are paired up with experienced mediators for their early experience in the field.

The aims of the training programme of one service in Wales are reflected in those of all the programmes:

- to cover the entire mediation process from first contacts through to closure and review
- to create a solid foundation in fundamental mediation skills such as active listening
- impartiality, trust building, prejudice reduction, managing conflict and facilitating negotiation
- to develop an understanding of mediators' own responses to conflict, so that they can manage their own feelings and assumptions, and interact constructively with disputants
- to enhance an understanding of disputes and dispute behaviour
- to address issues of equality of opportunity at all stages.

A mediation project in East London responsible for training volunteers is compiling its own Training Manual combining the skills training in the Mediation UK Manual and need for understanding between the many different cultures represented in the local community. The programme opens with work about people handling conflict creatively in their own lives, drawing on people's own experiences of conflict. It aims to help people to grow in confidence and to handle their own conflicts and emotions as a foundation on which to build the skills which they will require to mediate in disputes between neighbours from many cultural traditions.

In 24 community mediation services which gave numbers trained within the previous twelve months in courses they themselves delivered, a total of 491 volunteers had completed training.

Some issues arising from the training of volunteer mediators are of similar concern to all services which use volunteers, such as victim support, Relate, befriending schemes and advice services. In the first place, there is concern about recruitment. One service asserts that 'Broadly speaking all mediation services recruit and train local people . . .' and all would agree that mediators with an inside knowledge of local community issues are likely to empathise most closely with the aspirations of disputants. Services hope to recruit a balanced team including women and men of all age groups and all cultural groups in their communities. A service wants to be able to depend on local people coming forward for training but it also wants to attract those who have the right qualities to be successful mediators and who will justify the investment of resources put into training them. For example, the East London service asks its volunteers to make a commitment to a minimum of 100 hours involvement a year, which may include management committee meetings and further training as well as casework. Some respondents commented that volunteers were slow in coming forward. Recruitment campaigns on local radio and in the local press and public advertising spaces bring little response. Local educational establishments are better recruiting grounds, but students are transient and often are newcomers to the area. While many community mediation services are necessarily dependent on volunteer mediators, and would prefer to remain so, one well-established service has moved away from recruitment of volunteers to the paid employment of a few former tried and tested ones who have proven high quality performance.

On the issue of accreditation, one respondent robustly declared, 'We strongly affirm that qualifications are given to courses by participants not to participants by course organizers'. While this indicates faith in the participants, it does not say anything about how they were chosen or their effectiveness as mediators. Generally, however, there is momentum towards acquiring accreditation for training and this external scrutiny will be welcomed by clients wanting assurance of quality. While the East London trainer does not wish her training to become over academic and achievement orientated, she is seeking accreditation from the local Open College Network to give her programme credibility in the eyes of clients and funders. She acknowledges that while pressure to achieve qualified status may be off-putting to some volunteers, others welcome it personally as a positive asset in the search for employment and there is general recognition that the credibility of the service will be enhanced if there is public awareness that mediators are trained and qualified for the job.

Some experienced practitioners argue that there should be more rapid progress towards a nationally recognised qualification for mediators. This should include a balance of theoretical and practical proficiency; theory is needed and provides helpful background but it cannot address the practical issues which only emerge from experience. One co-ordinator with many years' experience in the field would like to see a Mediation UK led recognised qualification for a generic mediator incorporating basic training and a probationary period of supervised practice. This would compare with the training procedures required by Relate, which relies on volunteer counsellors for the delivery of its service.

TRAINING IN SPECIALISED FIELDS

The discussion so far has focused on the training of volunteer mediators in basic mediation skills suitable for practising mediation in neighbourhood disputes, described by one respondent as 'a niche version of broad skills'. For work in other fields of mediation and alternative dispute resolution, additional, field-specific training is required. For example, community mediation services which expand into or specialise in victim-offender mediation, add training focused on the criminal justice process, working with young offenders, the problems faced by victims of crime and casework experience shadowing mediators in the field. Mediation UK has drawn together good practice in *Victim-Offender Mediation Guidelines* but again there is no accredited qualification for a volunteer or professional taking a course. In the Scottish Mediation and Reparation project described in *Chapter 6*:

> People wishing to become mediators are not automatically recruited. Great care and attention to detail is given in the final selection of volunteers before and after completion of the induction training course.

The Mediation Induction Training Programme runs for 12 weeks covering all aspects of the scheme from product knowledge to the role of the mediator within the context of reparation. On completion of the course, top-up training is delivered weekly as an ongoing development for volunteers and staff, dealing with individual and group training needs as identified through job evaluation and monitoring. Volunteers are given regular and structured support and supervision and case review meetings are held at regular intervals in order to assess practitioner skills.

The level of commitment of the ten active volunteers in this scheme is clearly of a high order.

Peer mediation schemes in schools, as illustrated in *Chapter 7*, demand specialised training to suit the needs of the children involved and to support the adults, teachers and parents alike, of the whole school community. Mediation UK acts as a network for schools-based schemes and has produced briefing and conference papers to assist services wanting to initiate work in this as yet limited field of activity.

Family Mediation training
The training requirements for family mediators have been developed by the organizations involved in this field to meet the extra demands, emotional, legal and procedural, which cases involve. Only one of the family mediation services out of 20 responding to the questionnaire uses volunteers, reflecting the professional nature of mediation in this field. In order to establish the professional status of family mediation, National Family Mediation (NFM), the Family Mediators Association (FMA) and Family Mediation Scotland have together founded the UK College of Family Mediators with the following objects:

- to advance the education of the public in the skills and practice of mediation
- to set, promote, improve and maintain the highest standards of professional conduct and training for those practising in the field of family mediation; and
- to make available the details of registered mediators qualified to provide family mediation.

The college will establish a register of nationally recognised professional mediators, who have satisfied its training and supervised practice requirements, who will respond to the expansion of family mediation which the Family Law Act 1996 will generate: see *Chapter 4*.

In its statement of Professional and Organizational Requirements, National Family Mediation outlines the selection, training, supervision and accreditation procedures by which it provides a national framework for protecting uniform standards of professional practice for family mediation. The National Core Training Programme includes understanding of the legal, ethical, social and psychological context in which family mediation occurs as well as an understanding of mediation as a process and the core skills of mediation. Full accreditation is gained by the family mediator after completing the programme: at least one year's work with 75 hours face-to-face mediation experience, 15 summaries of case outcomes and an evaluation booklet completed by mediator and supervisor, rating competence in a range of skills and professional development.

Many family law solicitors and some barristers have reacted to the growing demand for mediation by ensuring that they are trained in mediation skills and able to act for separating and divorcing couples both as mediators and legal advisers under the provisions of the Family Law Act. The Solicitors Family Law Association (SFLA) has sponsored 'a training faculty of lawyers and experienced mediators from other disciplines to run training courses nationally' in mediation training for lawyers.

> The training programme is intended to provide a good theoretical understanding of mediation process and communication skills, a sound practical and ethical base for practice, an understanding of the personal and emotional issues facing couples entering into mediation and the integration of existing expertise and practice with new ways of working. It will be geared to sole mediation (which is likely to be the approach favoured by the Lord Chancellor's Department) but it will also include co-mediation so that practitioners will be able to co-mediate when they consider this appropriate.

Mediators completing the course will be provisionally accredited by the SFLA and able to mediate; after two years experience and a further 160 hours of training, counselling, peer group discussion and practice, they will be able to apply for full accreditation. The SFLA is working with the Law Society to agree minimum standards for solicitor family mediators, and their training programme provides 'accreditation and regulation within a framework of consultancy and further education criteria and requirements being discussed and agreed with the Law Society'.

The depth of knowledge and skills required for family mediation and the demands shortly to be made on the service have transformed what began as a service provided by the voluntary sector into a highly professionalised one. The development of family mediation services was described in more detail in *Chapter 4*.

OTHER ADR TRAINING

Mediation and conflict resolution training amongst professionals other than lawyers who are involved in such work is patchy. Organizations and agencies which responded that conflict resolution is part of their activity sometimes have relevant courses or workshops as part of their in-service training programmes, and sometimes not. For example, some probation services, social services and police forces have some related training on a range of topics such as handling conflict and aggression, negotiation skills, team building and dispute resolution. Some of the training is designed to enhance the ability of staff to handle issues internal to their organization as well as in their work with their client group. Housing departments and Housing Associations have few training programmes in these areas, preferring to refer tenant disputes to a local community mediation service.

Trade Unions run education programmes for their members, and especially for their activists, in negotiating and bargaining skills and procedures associated with disciplinary and grievance proceedings. For example, UNISON course books for shop steward training include information and practical activities on all aspects of negotiating and pay bargaining, including strategies for negotiating with management and dispute procedures. In the field of commercial mediation, CEDR and the ADR Net Limited have become major providers of training. The ADR Net specialises in training lawyers in the skills of mediation and other ADR strategies. CEDR provides a range of courses on dispute resolution, dispute avoidance and conflict management and will also tailor courses to meet the requirements of particular organizations and situations, such as 'Managing Conflicts in the Charities Sector' and 'Complaints Handling'. The aim of the training organizations is to establish a high standard of practice and recognition of the professionalism of those who gain their accreditation and many of the courses are recognised by the Law Society as part of Continuing Professional Development.

The Chartered Institute of Arbitrators is the governing body for professional arbitrators. To achieve associate membership and eligibility for appointment as an accredited arbitrator, candidates must attend courses and pass different levels of its examination and other continuing education requirements, with an emphasis on relevant law.

THE TRAINERS

Trainers of mediation and ADR skills should be experienced practitioners and trained trainers. In the early days of neighbourhood mediation when local groups were forming, often the training was based on a guide or manual and mediators learnt primarily 'on the job', building up expertise from practice. Now there are mediators with training and experience who pass on their skills to new groups of volunteers, though the co-ordinator of a well-established service expressed concern that as yet there is no national accreditation scheme for trainers of mediation.

National Family Mediation training is provided nationally by a team of trainers and presenters. Supervisors of newly trained family mediators must themselves have some current practice and have been trained or be willing to be trained by NFM in mediation supervision.

The SFLA is establishing its standards within the professional framework of the Law Society, which has a register of over 100 authorised Continuing Professional Development Providers of ADR courses nationwide. With the growth in demand for mediation and ADR and the increasing diversity in the fields where it is practised, freelance trainers working individually or in consortia are increasing in number. Mediation UK is in the process of setting up a Directory of organizations and individuals offering training in mediation and ADR skills.

An overall picture
Questionnaires (*Chapter 3*) were sent out to a sample of 30 training organizations of which 53 per cent responded. These could be divided into generic trainers, who offered mediation and conflict resolution skills broadly based on the Mediation UK Training Manual or other models discussed below, and 'niche trainers', who offered training in a particular field of activity. Niche trainers who responded included large organizations such as the family mediation specialists and the commercial specialists and smaller organizations focusing on work with young people, including youth justice and peer mediation, victim-offender mediation and inter-faith and intra-faith mediation. These smaller organizations overlap with a group of initiatives which focus on helping groups and individuals to understand and tackle conflict within their own experience. Some of these groups, especially those working with young people, use the arts as a vehicle for creatively dealing with conflict and facilitating conflict resolution.

Two such organizations come from Quaker roots. The Alternatives to Violence Project (AVP) is 'an organization of volunteers who, through running workshops, enable people to develop effective ways of dealing with conflict creatively and without violence.' AVP began in 1975 as a project supported by local Quakers to help violent young people in prisons in New York State. The project spread throughout the

United States and beyond, and from 1990 AVP groups, involving people of all faiths and none, have been running workshops in the community as well as in prisons in many parts of Britain. Through exercises and discussion, AVP workshops

> build on everyday experience and try to help people move away from violent behaviour by developing conflict resolution skills. The basis of the Alternatives to Violence Project is a belief that there is a power for peace and good in everyone, and that this power can transform violence . . . Participants are encouraged to look within themselves and their own experience for solutions to conflict.

LEAP Confronting Conflict, founded in 1987, evolved from the work of the Leaveners, the Quaker performing arts project. It was initiated in response to concern about growing youth unemployment and crime rates to explore the causes and alternatives to conflict through drama and theatre. The project works with young people at risk and with youth and community groups and workers, offering a range of workshops and creative experiences in which participants explore strategies for confronting conflict non-violently and meeting anger and confrontational behaviour with a range of conflict resolution techniques.

Another respondent in this group was the National Coalition Building Institute (NCBI), a community training organization which originated in Washington DC and spread to Canada, Switzerland and the UK during the last 15 years. NCBI claims to be unique in its training approach, offering models for training the skills of prejudice reduction, inter-group conflict resolution and coalition building which aim to build active teams of community leaders to replicate the programme in local centres.

> NCBI workshops and training events teach replicable models which use emotional healing to reduce prejudice and to resolve inter-group conflict. The diversity among the participants provides a powerful training experience which is enhanced by opportunities to learn in small training groups. Participants are encouraged to share and take pride in their own background and experiences, while developing more effective tools for the eradication of all bigotry . . .
> Community leaders who have been through the Leadership Training meet regularly and use the NCBI models to lead prejudice reduction programmes and to intervene in tough community conflicts . . . Our vision is to have an NCBI trained community resource team based in every major city and town in the country.

NCBI training is challenging in its approach and aims to be empowering, though its model and methods of confronting emotional issues sometimes generate controversy. Some participants in NCBI programmes feel that they move too quickly and are too prescriptive and American in their cultural assumptions that everyone is ready to make intensely personal disclosures. For others, the programme is a powerful, challenging and enlightening experience and they would welcome more collaborative events with NCBI trainers working in local settings.

The UK Regional Director explained that NCBI has to be prescriptive because any alteration or use of only part of the programme out of context would undermine the integrity of the whole. For example, the healing work in the Prejudice Reduction Workshop underpins the whole programme and is essential to it. The programmes are vehicles for people to move beyond their daily interactions in order to get close to and work with people different from themselves. The UK Director shares the NCBI vision of wanting to change the world to make every community inclusive where all feel welcome. NCBI leaders complete the full programme of training in Prejudice Reduction and Conflict Resolution before they become accredited to work in pairs to lead workshops using the centrally-produced training materials. Leaders receive constant support and supervision and regular top-up training to reinforce their skills. The UK Director emphasised the high level of skill needed by leaders in order to deliver the model effectively.

Some independent training organizations are profit-making and some cost-covering not-for-profit; either way they charge for their services. Highest rates are set for industrial or business clients, with more moderate fees for voluntary organizations and lower rates for individuals, especially those on benefit. Rates for residential courses as would be expected are higher than for day workshops and seminars.

There are inherent dangers in the open and only partially structured stage of development of training in mediation and conflict resolution. Opportunist trainers may take advantage of the demand to market courses which are based on superficial theoretical knowledge and inadequate or unsuccessful practice in the field. Groups and individuals seeking training should examine the credentials of trainers with care before joining courses or commissioning training programmes. The issue of recognised standards and qualifications for trainers urgently needs to be resolved.

Prescriptive or elicitive model

Having reviewed the various training opportunities available in ADR, it is useful to reflect on them in relation to Lederach's comparison of the prescriptive and elicitive models. In Lederach's analysis of prescriptive training, the expert brings his or her own programme into the participants' setting. He or she controls the design and content of the training package and the progression from the introductory level to the specialised, advanced level. The goal of the training is the attainment of a credit or qualification or certificate of competence which proves that the participant has understood and mastered the model and thereby achieved qualified and professional status.

Lederach contrasts the prescriptive model with the elicitive model in which the focus switches away from the expertise of the trainer to the implicit knowledge and experience of the participants, who become the primary resource for the training. By concentrating on a process of discovery and by allowing participants to create their own techniques and strategies based on their own experience and cultural traditions, the elicitive model empowers them to pursue areas of conflict transformation appropriate to their needs. The model draws on the work of Paulo Freire and his concept of 'conscientization' or 'awareness-of-self-in-context' and the 'power of naming the world'.

Lederach argues that most training in conflict resolution is a mixture of the prescriptive and the elicitive and that both approaches are of value.

> Both models can create dynamic education to empower people, but do so from a different basis. The prescriptive approach empowers participants inasmuch as they learn and master new ways, techniques and strategies for facing and handling conflict. The elicitive pursues empowerment as validating and building from resources that are present in the setting.

He suggests, however, that the elicitive approach has benefits in being more culturally aware and more appropriate for the content of conflict transformation training. Much of the training described in this chapter seems to be at the prescriptive end of the spectrum. With the increasing emphasis on the importance of assessment, accreditation and professional qualifications, training programmes tend to become more cognitive-based and achievement orientated. There are, however, trainers with the voluntary sector who are aware of the value of the elicitive model, especially in settings where cultural issues are significant ingredients of conflict situations. A balance needs to be struck especially in community mediation between the need for accreditation to give credibility and quality assurance to the service and the need for openness to diversity and respect for participants as sources of knowledge and experience.

CONCLUSION

The variety of training opportunities and models is as diverse as fields of activity. One example of the search for training involves a woman in who was amazed at the number of courses on offer. Within 12 months, she had attended a workshop at the local university, an AVP weekend, a NCBI day seminar, a visit to the local Family Mediation Service, a UNESCO-sponsored seminar, and a two day course on victim-offender reparation and four days of mediation skills training, both the last offered by the local community mediation service. As a result, she is now in process of training to become an accredited volunteer in the community mediation service. Diversity does suit a wide variety of potential learners. However, it raises issues about commonality of perception about what mediation training should involve and what safeguard and standards need to be set up to protect students and practitioners and establish the status and reliability of trainers.

SOURCES AND FURTHER READING: *Chapter 12*

Cohen, R., *Students Resolving Conflict*, Goodyear Books, 1995
Crawley, J., *Constructive Conflict Management: Managing to Make a Difference*, 1992
Freire, P., *Pedagogy of the Oppressed*, 1972
Kingston Friends, *Introduction to Mediation*, 1991
Lederach, J.P., *Preparing for Peace: Conflict Transformation Across Cultures*, 1995
Mediation UK, *Training Manual in Community Mediation Skills*, 1996
Mediation UK, *Victim and Offender Mediation Handbook*, 1994
Moore, C., *The Mediation Process: Practical Strategies for Resolving Conflict*, 1986.

Acknowledgments
Mediation UK
Kingston Friends
National Family Mediation
Cardiff Mediation Service
Newham Conflict and Change
Derby Mediation Service
Sandwell Mediation Service
Grampian Reparation and Mediation Project
Solicitors' Family Law Association
Unison
Transport and General Workers' Union
Centre for Dispute Resolution (CEDR)
ADR Net
Alternatives to Violence Project
Leap Confronting Conflict
National Coalition Building Institute UK.

CHAPTER 13

Academic Study and Research

Conflict and conflict resolution are areas of growing interest to students in higher education and to researchers and there is a wide range of academic activity, all of which contributes to the enhancement of theoretical knowledge and to the pursuit of excellence in practice. This chapter uses responses to the questionnaires (*Chapter 3*) to examine the diversity of research and the range of courses. Themes which might be explored in future research projects are outlined and comments made about the overarching framework for the study of conflict resolution.

RESEARCH

Fifty-nine respondents (29.3 per cent) answered 'Yes' to the question 'Are you or your organization doing research in this area?' 25 (43 per cent) of these were voluntary organizations, 24 (40 per cent) were from the statutory sector, six (10 per cent) were private, non-profit organizations and four (7 per cent) were private and profit-making. Eleven out of a total of 60 responses from community mediation services registered that they were involved in relevant research projects but a wide variety of other voluntary organizations indicated that they undertake work in this area in order to be able and evaluate and improve their practice:

Community mediation services	11
Family mediation services	3
Trade unions	2
Victim-offender projects	2
Victim support schemes	1
Education projects	2
Relate (+ Relate Family Studies Centre)	1
Youth training	1
CVS	1
Advocacy group	1

Table 13.1: Voluntary Organizations Engaged in Research Activity

The type of research in progress in the projects listed above and in the private, non-profit making organizations, can broadly be classified as:

	Voluntary	Private, non-profit making
Action research	8	2
Monitoring and evaluation		
of outcomes	11	2
Policy issues	4	2
Feasibility/comparative		
studies	2	

Table 13.2: Types of Research Activity

Action research projects include:

- studies of the relationship between neighbourhood disputes and infrastructure (children's play space, soundproofing etc.)
- the relationship between neighbourhood disputes and people's health
- conflict resolution strategies appropriate to different cultural traditions
- longitudinal studies of family mediation
- creative work with young people involved in street gangs.

Research based on the monitoring and evaluation of projects includes studies of outcomes of mediation, and client satisfaction with agreements achieved by family mediation. Policy issues include the development of ways of handling anti-social behaviour, and research into criminal justice policy practice by the Howard League for Penal Reform.

In nine instances, voluntary and non-profit organizations are working collaboratively with other agencies; seven of these partnerships are with academic institutions such the project on the cost-effectiveness of neighbourhood mediation from the Centre for Criminology and Legal Research at Sheffield University and Mediation UK and two community mediation services referred to in *Chapter 6*. Research by Relate is based at the Centre for Family Studies at Newcastle University. Mediation UK through its quarterly publication *Mediation* keeps its membership abreast of research projects and their findings.

Research in conflict resolution in the statutory sector is department-orientated. The positive responses to research activity came from a spread of agencies:

Police	6
Probation services	3
Home Office	1
Social services	2
Housing department	1
ACAS/Ombudsman	4
Civil court service	1
Universities	6

Table 13.3: Research Activity in Statutory Agencies

Research relating to victim-offender and reparation projects is located in projects led by the police and probation services, with broad oversight from the Home Office. Academic support comes from the Centre for Criminological and Legal Research at Sheffield and the Institute for the Study and Treatment of Delinquency at King's College, London. The multi-disciplinary Diversion Unit whose work is described in *Chapter 6* is engaged in a number of small research projects within the unit and also collaborating with the local college on a more detailed examination of the outcomes of its programme. The West Yorkshire Probation service project described in *Chapter 6* was evaluated in 1990 by the Home Office; despite and indeed because of current financial constraint, it needs to continue to evaluate its work:

> We are aware that our future depends on outcomes which can show that mediation and reparation and other victim perspective work influences attitudes and behaviour of offenders. We will be engaged in a further research project with our research and information section here in West Yorkshire Probation Service, looking long term at the impact of our intervention on the reconviction rate of offenders.

Research projects from county police forces include the effects of community policing and the monitoring and evaluation of new initiatives in the Thames Valley area to educate young shoplifters to prevent them from reoffending.

Research relating to conciliation work with families comes from the Centre for Family Studies at Newcastle, and from social services departments, an example of which is the development of Family Group Conferences described in *Chapter 4*, piloted by Hampshire Social Services and evaluated by the Social Services Research and Information Unit at Portsmouth University.

In the fields of commercial and industrial conflict resolution, positive evidence from trade unions and professional associations, ACAS, ombudsmen, the Central London County Court and two firms of solicitors demonstrates that this area too attracts research activity. For example, a solicitor engages in 'general research, primarily to enhance our insurance-based litigation', while the collection and publication of statistical data by trade unions, resumés circulated by professional associations and articles in journals such as the *Law Society Gazette* ensure that information about new research initiatives of interest to the commercial lawyer is disseminated.

Training organizations are also engaging in research, examples being work on 'Neighbours, Nuisance and Mediation', 'Gender Difference in Listening and Rapport Building as Mediators', and evaluation of the use of video and drama in work with victims and offenders.

Specialist departments

There are a few university departments which specialise in the study of peace, conflict and conflict resolution which deserve special mention. They include the Department of Peace Studies at Bradford University.

> The Department of Peace Studies at the University of Bradford was established in 1973 following an initiative from the Society of Friends [Quakers]. It is still the only university department in Britain concerned exclusively with the study of peace, and remains the largest university centre of its kind in the world, offering a full programme of undergraduate and postgraduate programmes . . .
>
> There are over 30 full-time research students from many countries . . . Three interlinked groups develop the department's research in the areas of international security, conflict resolution and politics and society . . .
>
> The primary objectives of the research group on conflict resolution, mediation and peace-keeping are to undertake research into the causes of conflict and the means by which it can be peacefully resolved . . . While the research agenda of the group is broadly based and includes research into situations of local and domestic conflict, and on the history of the thinking and practice of peacemaking, the core emphasis is placed on understanding how the various agencies of the international community can maximise and co-ordinate their potential to enhance conflict resolution outcomes when they intervene in a major conflict.

There is also a second specialist department in Northern Ireland:

> The Centre for the Study of Conflict is a research centre of the University of Ulster which carries out research investigations, all of which are financed by outside funders. It concentrates on questions to do with peace, conflict studies and ethnic relations, and is the largest research-oriented centre dealing with these matters in Ireland. In the past much of its work focused on the Northern Ireland conflict, but it is currently developing a range of comparative and international dimensions.

The action research on peer mediation in primary schools described in *Chapter 7* is a project within the Centre for the Study of Conflict. Recent research within Northern Ireland has focused on the phenomenon of parading, analysing the conflicts surrounding parades and possible approaches to resolving them. International projects involve collaborative work with teams of researchers in South Africa, Israel and New York; this international dimension has been enhanced by the establishment in Derry of the Peace Department of the United Nations University (UNU).

The Initiative on Conflict Resolution and Ethnicity—INCORE—has been established since 1993 as the Peace Department of UNU to provide the research and training facilities required to support the efforts of the United Nations to mediate in ethnic conflicts.

INCORE's central aims are to increase understanding of the origins, dynamics and effects of ethnic conflict, and to encourage better approaches to conflict management and resolution. Its principal methods of accomplishing these aims are research and training.

The research strategy has been developed directly from INCORE's identification of the importance of specific phases in the development of ethnic conflict. Its emphasis is on the management of ethnic diversity and the problems associated with rebuilding social, economic and political structures after phases of violence. In addition, reflecting the link to the United Nations through the UNU, there is a commitment to providing research support for the United Nations and other international agencies. This implies flexibility in research planning and a willingness to respond to specific needs, particularly in areas of policy-related research. As a result, INCORE's research activities reflect a balance between long term goals and the need to meet more immediate requests.

INCORE has its base on the Magee Campus of the University of Ulster in Derry, chosen because it offered the opportunity of observing a cultural conflict at close quarters. While the local conflict can be used as a case study, all INCORE research projects must be comparative and must have an international dimension. Its current projects focus on the themes of peacekeeping and the peace processes which establish the structures for maintaining peace in the future between communities moving away from an open conflict situation. The Peace Process Project is working on a four-year programme of comparative case studies from South Africa, Palestine, Sri Lanka, Yugoslavia and the Basque country on the Spanish/French border. As new projects attract funding, research outposts will be established in or near areas of ethnic conflict to provide more data for comparative work.

INCORE is developing a sophisticated data centre 'to support and co-ordinate research by making available for policy makers, researchers and the media, information and access to information on ethnic conflict and conflict resolution.' This is growing alongside the Ethnic Studies Network already set up by practitioners and researchers in ethnic conflict as a result of the initiative of the Centre for the Study of Conflict.

The International Institute of Peace Studies and Global Philosophy is investigating the possibility of becoming the core of a Peace Studies Centre for first degree and graduate studies in the University of London. Meanwhile it is operating as a voluntary body alongside the university. It provides a network of research and information on peace studies worldwide and publishes an academic international journal 'dedicated to education and research into the positive dynamics of building global peace and justice through love'.

Undergraduate courses
Although a number of other universities offer opportunities for postgraduate work in conflict resolution, courses at first degree level are more difficult to track down. Any list of courses needs constant checking as new modules are constantly being written in and published ones lapse. Apart from modules in conflict resolution in the BA Peace Studies courses at Bradford University, opportunities for first degree students to study ADR are almost exclusively to be found as modules in law courses for undergraduates. However, the flexibility of some social science courses allows for a choice of subject for extended essays or dissertations. For example, recent students on the BA course in Youth and Community Work at Derby University have elected to study themes such as the use of mediation in resolving neighbourhood disputes and the place of volunteers in mediation services.

Future research in conflict resolution and ADR
The above shows that a variety of issues are being researched by a wide variety of agencies, both academic and in the field. Research into ethnic conflict and peace studies at international level seems to be well covered and well co-ordinated. The greatest concentration of research into conflict resolution in domestic society appears to be in the areas of restorative justice and family mediation, with neighbourhood mediation and schools work attracting less investigation. In all fields in the UK, levels of research activity have a long way to go to match the outpourings of material in the United States.

If and when resources are available, there is no lack of topics, themes, problems and questions which beg for research. For example, the Sheffield research on the cost-effectiveness of mediation in neighbour disputes concluded 'that by probing the issues we have simply established how little we know about the problem, and how much more is still to be done'. Five further possible topics for research into neighbour disputes are suggested by Sheffield, including more sophisticated examination of cost comparisons and a survey of comparative consumer satisfaction. Other topics in neighbour mediation that have been suggested by practitioners in the field are research into different, culture-specific models of conflict healing strategies; a comparison of attitudes to and outcomes of face-to-face and indirect mediation; and an enquiry into long-term outcomes of mediation, comparing, for example, the level of police intervention required in a neighbourhood with an active mediation service with the level needed in a neighbourhood without a mediation service.

Although there has been rigorous research in the field of restorative justice, Tony Marshall has identified a number of directions for further research which would strengthen the case for bringing victim-offender mediation into mainstream practice, such as more investigation of the relative effectiveness of direct and indirect mediation; research into the impact of victim-offender mediation on re-offending rates; enquiry into victim satisfaction; and measurement of attitude change in offenders.

In schools work, research is needed to measure the effectiveness of peer mediation as an agent of change in whole school ethos. Monitoring of programmes is needed to demonstrate the benefits of including the adult community of the school in the training programme. Comparative studies are required to measure the impact of peer mediation schemes on levels of playground bullying. The benefits of peer mediation training to individual pupils in terms of growth in confidence and levels of achievement also need to be monitored and evaluated.

The implementation of outstanding parts of the Family Law Act 1996 from 1999 will call for monitoring and research into the benefits, cost-effectiveness and client satisfaction of family mediation. New models such as Family Group Conferences need more research as do projects in fields such as ageism and disability where mediation strategies are in an early stage of development. Possibilities for conflict resolution in environmental disputes need the impetus of exploratory research. Mediation in the gay community has been suggested as a new area for enquiry.

All these areas of research have been suggested either by practitioners in the field or by researchers currently engaged in projects. Some concern was expressed that enthusiasm for individual research projects means competition for limited funding and obscures the need for coherent development of an overarching philosophical and ethical framework for conflict resolution within which priorities can be established. Although the ever-increasing range and diversity of activity is invigorating and challenging to researchers, the strength to be gained from commonality of vision and solidarity of purpose is recognised and desired. Mediation UK is currently the most inclusive focus of conflict resolution practice and research in the UK and does a magnificent job of co-ordination; a coalition of all interests and all fields is needed to provide a research, information and resource centre for domestic conflict resolution studies.

DEGREE COURSES

The following list, compiled from university prospectuses, gives a broad spectrum of the variety of opportunities available for the study of conflict resolution and related issues at degree level and for research. New courses, and new modules within existing courses, are continually being developed, and at the same time existing courses are modified; current prospectuses should therefore be consulted to check details.

FIRST DEGREE COURSES

Aberdeen University, Law Department, option in 'Alternative Methods of Dispute Resolution'.
University of Abertay, Dundee, Law Department, option in 'Industrial Tribunal Law'.
Anglia Polytechnic University, Community Studies, module on 'Images and Rhetoric of Conflict'. Law Department: 'Skills in Negotiation and Advocacy'.
Queen's University, Belfast, Law Department: option 'Dispute Resolution'; workshop on 'Negotiation'.
Bradford University, Department of Peace Studies, options include 'Conflict Resolution', 'UN Peacekeeping and Intervention', 'Northern Ireland', 'Culture Recognition and Conflict', 'Conflict Resolution in International Society'.
De Montfort University, Leicester, has an Institute for the Study of War and Society.
Essex University, Law Department: 'International Peacekeeping'.
University of Glamorgan, Law Department: HND Legal Studies includes 'Alternative Dispute Resolution'.
Hull University, Law Department: 'Conflict Resolution Options'.
University of Kent, Department of Politics and International Relations, option in 'Conflict Theory'.
Kingston University, Law Department, option of 'Negotiation Workshops'.
Lancaster University, Department of Applied Science, option include 'Victim-Offender Mediation' and 'Family Group Conferencing'.
London School of Economics, Law Department, options include 'Alternative Dispute Resolution'.
University of Nottingham, Sociology Department, modules on 'Conflict and Controversy in Contemporary Britain'.

University of Plymouth, 'International Relations'; units on 'Theories of Conflict', 'Conflict Resolution' and 'Peacekeeping'.

University of Reading, Department of Politics and International Relations, option of 'War, Peace and International Ethics'. Department of Sociology: unit on 'Sociology of Conflict and Conflict Resolution'.

South Bank University, Law Department, option on 'Alternative Dispute Resolution'.

University of Westminster, Law Department, optional modules include 'Alternative Dispute Resolution'.

University of Plymouth, International Relations, units on 'Theories of Conflict and Conflict Resolution and on Peacekeeping'.

SECOND DEGREE AND RESEARCH

Bradford University, Department of Peace Studies.

University of Durham, Departments of Law, Politics and Sociology and Social Policy.

International Institute of Peace Studies and Global Philosophy at London University Institute of Education.

King's College, London, Institute for the Study and Treatment of Delinquency.

Queen Mary and Westfield College, London, Department of Politics.

Loughborough University, Social Sciences Department and Centre for Research in Social Policy.

The Manchester Metropolitan University, INCOREC.

Newcastle University, Centre for Family Studies.

Nottingham Trent University, Law School.

Portsmouth University, Social Services Research and Information Unit.

Sheffield University, Centre for Criminology and Legal Research.

University of Ulster, Centre for Conflict Resolution.

The United National University of Ulster, Initiative on 'Conflict Resolution and Ethnicity'.

CHAPTER 14

Issues For The Future

The chapters of this book reveal a diversity and richness of conflict resolution which is invigorating and encouraging. It proved a considerable challenge to select from the wealth of information sent in response to the questionnaires (*Chapter 3*) and elicited from interviews representative examples with which to illustrate the overall outlines of the different fields of activity, and so as to keep within a balanced and concise framework.

In reviewing the fields of activity in which conflict resolution work is developing, the book began with the intensely personal conflicts within families. The scene shifted to the neighbourhood, school and world of work and commercial activity. Discussion of the applications of alternative dispute resolution within the criminal justice process opened up a contentious and highly emotive area. Issues of multi-cultural and multi-faith conflict resolution and ADR on environmental issues were separated for special discussion, but have common elements with conflicts in any of the other fields.

A significant message is that although each field of activity has its own special characteristic and concerns, they all share similar issues and processes and aim to keep those directly involved in a conflict in control of the solution. They are all underpinned by a shared ethos and a shared belief that non-violent, non-confrontational and non-adversarial resolution of conflict is both possible and desirable. They also have in common the search for a resolution and outcome which builds on

- *co-operation* rather than *competition*
- shared rather than opposed interests and values
- constructive rather than destructive ways forward
- transformation from hurt to healing.

Arising from the strong commonality running through all the fields of activity, there are some overarching issues which demand attention and consideration.

Networking and working in collaboration
Some community mediation services undertake work within several fields of activity and clearly perceive the interaction between these fields. One of the most obvious is the link between neighbourhood mediation and victim-offender mediation arising from the danger of the

neighbour dispute escalating into violence which involves police intervention and criminal prosecution. Work in schools, work with young people in clubs and on the streets and work with families all have direct relevance to work in neighbourhoods and to diversion projects using mediation as part of a strategy for changing behaviour patterns. In any of these fields, cultural diversity between the parties in dispute adds a dimension to the conflict which requires acknowledgement and insight on the part of the mediator.

Unsuspected commonality was discovered between the work of an ombudsman scheme, community mediation services and commercial mediation agencies. The consensus building work of environmental mediators is very similar in process to the work of commercial mediators and has resonance with the negotiations between trade unions and management, between tenants associations and landlords, or family group conferencing. The book gives examples of excellent interagency working between professional agencies, especially in victim-offender mediation, and some of collaborative work between voluntary organizations and professional agencies.

Successful conflict resolution depends on the facilitation of open dialogue on the basis of equality between all the interested parties, and projects in all fields can learn from knowing about each other's innovations and successes. Mediation UK acts as an impressive exchange point for ideas and news of developing projects but links with its major areas of concern are much stronger than with some other fields of activity. The untapped potential for collaborative work between organizations and across agencies is enormous and the benefits in terms of accessibility and efficiency to the user and in cost-effectiveness and growth in number of cases to the providing agency or organization incalculable. There is a need for more empirical research to provide the hard evidence which will encourage the establishment, monitoring and evaluation of more programmes and projects.

Diverse strategies of ADR
A further commonality between the fields of activity lies in the range of strategies used in conflict resolution. In no agency or organization and in no field of activity is only a single form of ADR used. The full range of strategies is exploited in many fields and all are using variants of similar approaches to resolve conflict, adapted to different situations to give best outcomes within the particular circumstances of the client group.

Again, practitioners can learn from each other's techniques, try out innovative strategies found effective in one situation in a different situation, share ideas and philosophies as well as the detail of proven good practice. In some localities a great deal of useful communication between projects produces fruitful growth. In some localities, innovative work happening in different fields of activity just round the corner from each other is *not* shared and new projects spend time and energy rediscovering for themselves ways of working that other projects are already using as routine.

Practical ways of working together

One obvious way forward is for representatives from all fields in a population centre to join in a local 'one-stop' conflict resolution service to which people could bring their disputes and problems. People are often uncertain where to go for help in a dispute situation—the local mediation service, the law centre, the CAB, the local council, a solicitor. Do they need a lawyer or a mediator, an arbitrator or a counsellor? People are not sure what each has to offer their particular situation or where to go to find exactly what they need. While the availability of information at local libraries can help, personal enquiry can be more accessible and effective. A 'one-stop' conflict resolution centre would provide a clearing house to advise the enquirer, either by phone or in person, of the options available for addressing their need and what each strategy could offer, from litigation through arbitration to mediation, from the prescriptive to the most informal. This would both raise the public's awareness of conflict resolution services and encourage them to use these services to their own benefit and the benefit of the community. A one-stop dispute centre in Boston, Massachusetts, offers information about all the different options available and where to find them, and clients can discuss the advantages and problems of each strategy of negotiating settlements, and what mixture of options can be used to reach the best solution in their particular situation.

Voluntary and professional ADR services

Conflict resolution services are offered through a wide variety of agencies distributed between two service sectors, voluntary and professional, with a growing contribution by the private sector added on. The voluntary sector is strong in most fields of activity and especially in neighbourhood mediation, victim-offender mediation, work in schools and with young people, multi-cultural and multi-faith mediation and family mediation. Many community mediation services work through volunteer mediators especially for neighbourhood disputes though there are also many paid mediators in voluntary organizations. Professional input also is strong in victim-offender mediation and family mediation with involvement from a variety of agencies including social work, education, health, probation services, police and the legal profession. There are some examples of excellent interagency working between professional agencies, especially in victim-offender mediation, and some of collaborative work between voluntary organizations and professional agencies.

There are many recently established private firms and consortia practising commercial mediation and offering mediation and ADR in other fields such as ombudsman schemes and environmental mediation, sometimes in association with lawyers. Unlike voluntary organizations and professional agencies, private firms charge fees for their services, though some on a non-profit making basis. The growth of interest from the legal profession in mediation and ADR is especially noticeable in the field of family mediation as well as in environmental and commercial mediation, in all of which legal considerations often provide a framework for disputes. Also in the workplace the complexities of employment law and health and safety law complicate the outcome of disputes and require professional expertise to disentangle.

A major issue for the future of conflict resolution is how the voluntary sector mediation services and professional practitioners of ADR can work alongside each other in ways that match the ethos of their service and offer maximum benefit to the community. Training forms the crucial terrain on which issues of voluntaryism and professionalism are contested. A professional has a formal, nationally recognised qualification gained by completing a course of study with academic and practice components and a period of probation in a related field. It may only be a matter of time before mediators in all fields are regulated by professional associations. The present situation of mediators can be compared to the pre-1825 state of solicitors who were then split between a number of different associations, which came together in 1825 to form The Law Society as the governing body of the whole profession (something pointed out by a respondent to the questionnaire).

Many community mediation services emphasise in their reports their perception of the value of an all-volunteer service. Many volunteer mediators are part of their local communities, some perhaps leading figures who have gained general respect as people to go to in a crisis. The rigorous and thoughtful training programmes, based on the Mediation UK model, which local mediation services deliver, are designed to provide adequate preparation to a volunteer with rich life experience and sound common sense. An all-volunteer Welsh service defines professionalism as:

- the ability to take work seriously, be prepared and on time and be respectful to parties at all time
- the willingness to efficiently undertake case recording, and monitoring, and the development of mediation competence
- the willingness to work as a member of a team, and with a co-worker
- the willingness to attend individual and group support and supervision sessions, to give and receive support.

While this describes professional qualities, without a recognised qualification community mediators may not be accorded the status of a full professional. In *Chapter 12* the variety of training opportunities in mediation skills was described and the movement towards accreditation of training courses recorded. But some volunteers from the community, who have much to offer, may feel excluded from becoming accredited mediators through deficit in previous educational record or unwillingness to engage in a long and demanding training process. The loss of such voluntary commitment and local expertise might damage the credibility of mediation in the eyes of many disputants who find a local community service accessible and friendly in contrast to a more formal bureau or office. There needs to be provision within accreditation schemes for accepting volunteers who are willing to undergo training and practise in a professional-like manner, but remain without formal qualifications, to continue to have a role within mediation services and be accepted as worthwhile practitioners. Comparable services which continue to use volunteers are Victim Support and Relate; Victim Support gives basic training locally backed up by a strong regional and national Victim Support training programme, while the training requirements for Relate counsellors are centralised and quite demanding.

For neighbourhood mediation services, professionalisation may seem a distant prospect but as accreditation becomes more widespread, as funders demand a higher standard of performance and as community mediation services spread their wings into new fields of activity such as schools work, victim-offender mediation, domestic violence, ageism and cross-cultural disputes, so the pressure to become more professionally structured is likely to increase.

The interest of solicitors and barristers in getting training in mediation skills is matched by the development of ADR modules in Law degrees noted in *Chapter 13*. As mentioned above, a takeover of the field of ADR by the law is confidently anticipated by some lawyers, which, to go by historical precedent, could end in ADR becoming as rule and procedure-bound as the law, with the possibility of the stifling of creativity that can come from control by one body which, some people might say, has primarily the interests of its membership at heart. An academic coming from a different perspective declared: 'It is time to reclaim conflict resolution for the humanities and liberal studies' and certainly in post-graduate research a number of social science and social policy departments are interested as well as specialist centres for the study of peace and/or conflict.

The issues of training and professionalism should not cause conflict between professional and amateur, prescriptive or elicitive approaches, accreditation or no accreditation or between different disciplinary backgrounds but should encourage sharing of ideas and experience and the building up of good practice. Policy for the development of professional training and standards can draw on excellence from all quarters, including good practice built on long experience such as that embodied in Mediation UK and examples from other countries with long experience in mediation such as the *Training Manual in Mediation* produced in 1996 by the Justice Institute of British Columbia which contains the following thoughts on developing professional standards:

> Umbreit (from the University of Minnesota) argues that the contemporary mediation movement is based on the ideals of neighbourhood empowerment and volunteerism. Mediator qualifications, certification and licensing lead away from these values, and may prevent many skilled volunteer mediators from being able to practice. The other side of the argument, as he lays it out, is that without some sort of regulation, the field is wide open to anyone wishing to call themselves a mediator, with all of the implied problems that situation causes to consumers and to the mediation field as a whole.
>
> Rifkin (in Folger and Jones, 1994) discusses the state of this emerging profession from the American point of view. She points out that more and more practising mediators have background in law, and are trained to view mediation as an extension of the legal system. In British Columbia there has been a concerted effort from mediation membership organizations and service providers to keep the field open to both lawyers and non-lawyers.
>
> The Society of Professionals in Dispute Resolution's Commission on Qualifications (with three Canadian members on the Commission), published in 1995 a report which attempted to balance 'the need to set standards, with a recognition that, because of the broad range of contexts in which dispute resolution occurs, defining a single set of standards could potentially limit and stifle the very skills, creativity and strengths that make this diverse field so valuable and rewarding.' Rather than articulate criteria or standards, they 'recommend a set of guidelines for policy makers, trainers, associations and others that help to organise the discussion of what in fact are the ingredients of competence for practitioners in the context within which they work.

This discussion shows that just as mediation and ADR was pioneered across the Atlantic before it spread to the UK, so the issues that are arising in the UK now have already been faced there and mediators in the UK can again learn from American and Canadian experience. The training model that seems to be evolving is made up of common core skills plus specific content and training for specific fields of activity, plus a period of supervised practice in the field. On the completion of each part of the training, a mediator receives accreditation and after completing the programme and assessment for competence in the chosen fields, the mediator is a qualified professional in those fields whether working as a volunteer or a paid employee. Conflict resolution practitioners from all fields need to agree some common approach to training to establish professional criteria and preserve the distinctiveness of ADR as a discipline before another discipline, predictably the law, steps in and swallows it up. They could, perhaps, learn from other professionals such as social workers, psychotherapists and youth workers to see how they faced comparable issues at similar stages of development.

Funding of ADR services
This book has not examined the sources of funding nor looked into the cost-effectiveness of services. While some of this has been the subject of research, more could well be focused on these issues. Impressionistic evidence suggests that all ADR is given low priority in budgets. Many community mediation services seem to live from hand to mouth, relying on a mixture of funding from local authority and housing association contracts, from health authorities, special initiatives such as Safer Cities and City Challenge and grants from charitable trusts. The project in East London which has been in existence for 13 years and is regarded as a leader in innovative good practice is uncertain of the continuation of funding for its development worker into the next financial year. A project in Nottingham funded by City Challenge for two years is unlikely to get any further funding and will depend for survival on the dedication of its small band of trained volunteers. Much of the extension of mediation into new areas of activity is funded on short term grants to voluntary projects.

In *Chapter 6* the lack of special funding in probation services for victim-offender mediation was discussed. Funding for family mediation following the implementation of the Family Law Act 1996 will come either from the clients or from legal aid. Ombudsmen in the public sector are funded from taxation, in the private sector from their members. Commercial mediators and private firms charge for their services. Trade union activities are funded by their membership. The funding for academic studies is not immune from the financial crises that universities are currently facing. The prospects for any rationalisation or increase in funding seem bleak but research to establish the cost-effectiveness of ADR might be a useful starting point.

Empowerment of people or professional agendas

Although the professionalisation of ADR seems inevitable, with collaborative effort, as has been suggested, this can be achieved in a way which establishes the distinctiveness of the discipline. Crucially, good practice in ADR must preserve the ethos of openness, fairness, equality, respect and the empowerment of people to make informed decisions about their own lives. Individuals and communities have enormous opportunities for exercising responsibility and practising active citizenship through participation in decision-making and problem-solving processes which contribute to the resolution of conflict. Issues of such empowerment were explored in discussion of the different fields of activity in which conflict resolution is developed; for example the empowerment of communities to engage in problem-solving justice and to make decisions about best use of resources to bring improvement to the harmony of a neighbourhood; the empowerment of children and young people to participate in decision-making about the rules governing their behaviour; the empowerment of families to make decisions about the future working of relationships; the empowerment of ordinary people to influence decisions about the future of the environment; the empowerment of citizens to fight decisions of government and corporations.

Alongside the use of conflict resolution strategies to redress the imbalance of power between parties in dispute, which is most tellingly demonstrated by work in the voluntary sector, the study has shown that professional and legal interest and involvement creates a more interventionist and structured approach which is unlikely to support and could well undermine the empowerment of ordinary people. This professionalisation of conflict resolution has been discussed with reference to neighbourhood, family and victim-offender work in particular. Dedicated practitioners are concerned at the power invested in the mediator which contradicts the empowering ethos of mediation. People in conflict situations often look to the mediator to find solutions and resolve their problems and it is all too easy for professionals working to excellent agendas to make judgments and subtly engineer what they perceive to be the right solutions. This is a temptation which must be avoided and the aim of the mediator must be to work with the disputants to enable them to use a conflict as a way to transform a relationship or a situation in such a way that the outcome is constructive and strengthening to themselves as individuals and to their families and communities. This is not to say that professional intervention and expert judgment are not appropriate and helpful in many situations, or that a quick arbitration of a dispute may not achieve the best outcome. Mediators must beware of making the assumption that mediation is always the answer; claiming too much for it could give it less credibility in those situations where it offers a powerful and transforming alternative.

The vision which seeks to strengthen the spiritual element in peacemaking should be grasped and assimilated to enrich all fields of conflict resolution. The role of academic study and research in formulating and expanding the theoretical and philosophical foundation of conflict resolution should be recognised and supported. The opportunities for students to include ADR as part of first degree studies and the facilities for research both need expansion and support. By fusing the experience and skills of the practitioner, the analytical methodology of the researcher and the vision of the philosopher, peace and conflict resolution studies in all fields could be enhanced and strengthened to the benefit of ordinary people and the world.

SOURCES AND FURTHER READING: *Chapter 14*

Folger, J. P. and Jones, T. S. (Eds.), *New Directions in Mediation: Communication Research and Perspectives,* 1994
Haddington, K., *Mediation Training Manual: Preliminary Draft,* Justice Institute of British Columbia, 1996
Umbreit, M., *Mediating Interpersonal Conflicts: A Pathway to Peace,* 1995.

Acknowledgements
All questionnaire respondents, and in particular:

Cardiff Mediation Service
Fife Mediation Service
Newham Conflict and Change
Sneighton/St. Ann's Mediation Service, Nottingham.

Appendix I: The Questionnaire

University of Nottingham

October 1996

Dear Colleague,

Conflict Resolution and Alternative Dispute Resolution

I am collecting information about current projects, courses and research in the field of conflict management—mediation, negotiation, ADR, conciliation etc.— with the aim of writing a Guidebook for students and practitioners.

As you will know well, conflict management in all its forms has 'taken off' as an area of practice, study and research over recent years. As a teacher of courses in Mediation and Conflict Resolution and working with colleagues at Derby Mediation Service, I have identified the need for a basic Guidebook to map the territory and give an overview of current development. In order to give as complete and as up-to-date a survey as possible I am relying on organizations and agencies such as yourselves to respond to this brief questionnaire. It would be most helpful if you could give as much detail as possible, if possible supplying any relevant literature with your response. The Guidebook will use all information received unless specifically marked 'not for publication'.

Please would you now help me in these ways:

* fill in the questionnaire, even if you have little or no information to offer;
* or pass it to another department or person to whom it may be relevant;
* **and return it by the end of November** (late responses still welcome).

Thank you very much for your help.

Yours sincerely,

Susan Stewart

Please return completed questionnaire using prepaid envelope.

Brief Outline of proposed Guidebook to Conflict Management:

Part One: Background and Concepts, historical, legal and sociological context, diversity of process, the practitioner

Part Two: The territory—neighbourhood, the family, victim-offender, industry and commerce, the individual and the state, peacemaking, the environment

Part Three: Training and the Future

Appendices: Analysis of questionnaires, current projects, courses, research.

1. NAME OF ORGANIZATION...

Address...

....

Contact person... Telephone number.............................

2. *Please circle the number which matches your organization:*

2a

1 Voluntary organization
2 Statutory/public
3 Private and profit making
4 Private, non-profit making

2b *Does the work of your organization include, broadly defined, conflict management/alternative dispute resolution?*   **YES/NO**

2c *Please circle the numbers which match your field of work:*

1 Neighbourhood mediation
2 Industrial/commercial mediation
3 Family mediation
4 Negotiation/conciliation services
5 Victim-offender mediation
6 Complaints/grievance procedures
7 Other ADR, please specify

3. *Please indicate type of work and numbers of workers:*

	Staff numbers:		Volunteer numbers:	
	full-time	part-time	full-time	part-time
Services				
Teach/train				
Research				
Publications				
Administration				

TOTAL

If details for questions 4-7 are given in accompanying literature, please tick 'Document'.

4. SERVICES   *Document* ....
Please describe the services you provide

5. RELEVANT TRAINING/COURSES

5a Does your organization deliver its own courses ?   **YES/NO**
Please complete numbers of participants per year:

	Staff	Volunteers	Students part-time	Students full-time	Accredited Y/N
Short					
Medium					
Long					

5b *Please list the courses that you deliver and specify qualifications gained for each:*
Document............

5c *Do your staff and/or volunteers attend courses outside your organization?*

Numbers per year............................ *Document*......................

5d *Courses your staff and/or volunteers attend:*
Please specify provider institution/agency and qualifications gained:

5e *Estimate of proportion of staff and volunteers who undertake training during a year:*

6. RESEARCH *Document*..............
Are you or your organization doing research in this area?　　YES/NO
Please give details

7. PUBLICATIONS *Document*............
Do you or your oganization publish in this area?　　YES/NO
Please give details

8. THE BOOK
Would 'A Guidebook to Conflict Management' be useful for:

your students?　　YES/NO
your staff?　　YES/NO
your volunteers?　　YES/NO

Have you any comments on this project or on the outline of the Guidebook?

9. *Would you be prepared to give further information or to have more discussion on any issue raised in this questionnaire by telephone or personal interview?*
YES/NO

Please feel free to take a photocopy of this document before you return it to the address shown on the front page.

THANK YOU VERY MUCH INDEED FOR YOUR CONTRIBUTION.

Appendix II: Methodology

The main findings of the research on which *Conflict Resolution: A Foundation Guide* is based are contained in *Chapter 3* and subsequent chapters. This appendix outlines the underlying *methodology*.

The questionnaire

As can be seen from *Appendix I*, a compact format was chosen for the questionnaire — so that respondents would be more likely to spend the relatively short time required to answer the questions. Advice was taken from experts in questionnaire technique on the working and layout having regard to clarity for the respondent, usability of the results for statistical calculations and facility of sorting and handling information. Some aspects of the responses are amenable to statistical analysis, some answers require qualitative assessment. From a small pilot run, the questionnaire was found to be serviceable with few amendments, and full distribution followed in November and December 1996.

Distribution

Questionnaires were sent to a large sample of specialist organizations involved in various fields of ADR and conflict resolution work. The collection of addresses for this part of the distribution was assisted by the publication in December 1996 of the new edition of the Mediation UK Directory which gives details of some groups which had hitherto been missed. An important objective of the research was to search out organizations in which ADR and conflict resolution activity takes place as strategy within their function and purpose. Questionnaires were therefore sent out to large samples of a wide variety of agencies and organizations. The table below gives details of the categories and the number of questionnaires sent out in each.

Category	No. of questionnaires sent	No. of returns	% returns
Specialist organizations			
Mediation/ADR services/			
projects	153	94	61%
Ombudsmen/legal services	22	12	54%
	175	106	60%
Non-specialist			
Social services departments	50	6	12%
Housing departments	30	3	10%
Probation services	40	8	20%
Universities	30	12	40%
Colleges	50	1	2%
Police	60	11	18%
Housing associations	85	13	15%
CVS/Voluntary Action	50	13	26%
Counselling, inc. Relate	40	11	27%
Religious organizations	30	7	23%
Trade unions	50	14	28%
	515	99	19%
Total	690	205	29.7%

Table: Questionnaire: Distribution and Responses

Range of responses

Seeking for conflict management in such a widespread and varied range of organizations and agencies produced a patchy response, but even where responses were thin, the quality of information returned was high.

Of the organizations responding, 57 per cent came from the voluntary sector, 26 per cent from the statutory sector and the remaining 17 per cent declared themselves to be private, dividing roughly equally between profit and non-profit-making. The response rate from the dedicated organizations was high, providing excellent insight into specialist fields of mediation and conflict resolution. The response from trade unions was lower than expected, as these are organizations, it might be supposed, which are crucially involved in the management and resolution of conflict and which might be expected to be open about their activities. The low response begs the question as to whether trade unions see themselves more as partisan organizations fighting their members' corner rather than active in the field of conflict resolution. The responses received were helpful and informative and provide a useful working sample.

The responses from statutory agencies were no lower than had been expected. For a questionnaire on a particular issue to reach the correct desk within a large and busy department is a matter of good fortune, and where information was forthcoming, with one exception, it covered the full range of agencies adequately and was indicative of concern to make use of multi-disciplinary approaches to conflict resolution.

Fourteen of the questionnaires to universities were directed to departments where relevant courses were known, from prospectuses, to be on offer. The response rate from these was disappointing though the detail of responses received from all universities compensated to some extent for their numbers. There was only one response from a sample of large colleges of higher and further education, probably because the questionnaire, as presented, did not seem relevant to the administrative staff who received it. It is difficult to believe that none of the colleges in the sample offers a course bearing on conflict or its management so it must be assumed that questionnaires failed to reach the right department or staff. Responses from religious organizations were also lower than antiicipated but those which give high priority to peace programmes responded with a wealth of information.

The letter accompanying the questionnaire (see *Appendix I*) requested a response even if it was negative. In reply to the question 'Does the work of your organization include, broadly defined, conflict management/alternative dispute resolution?' 18 (nine per cent) replied 'no'; eight of these were councils of voluntary service or umbrella voluntary action organizations, some of which supplied addresses of member organizations to which the questionnaire would be more relevant; three were religious organizations, three were housing associations and three were victim support groups which, as will be discussed later, do not define their role as within the field of conflict management.

Appendix III: List of Respondents

My thanks to the each of the following organizations, agencies and individuals who generously responded to the questionnaire reproduced in *Appendix I* and who between them provided the information which forms the basis of *Conflict Resolution: A Foundation Guide.*

Advisory, Conciliation and Arbitration Service (ACAS)
ACCORD, Cornwall
ADR Group
Alternatives to Violence Project, Sussex
Amber Valley Council for Voluntary Service
Association of British Insurers
Avon Probation Service
Bakers, Food and Allied Workers Union
Basildon College of Further Education
Bedfordshire Police
Bedfordshire Social Services
Birmingham Settlement
Bliss Mediation Service
Bournemouth Housing Association for the Elderly
Breckland Neighbourhood Mediation
Bridge Builders, London Mennonite Centre
Brighton Council for Voluntary Service
Brighton Victim Support
Bristol Family Mediation Service
Bristol Mediation
British Dental Association
Brixton Youth Activities Unit
Broadcasting Complaints Commission
Bromley Neighbourhood Mediation
Building Societies Ombudsman
Bully Free Zone, Bolton
Cambridge Community Mediation
Canterbury Mediation Service
Cardiff Mediation
Castle Morpeth Community Mediation
Centre for Dispute Resolution (CEDR)
Central London Court Service
Chartered Institute of Arbitrators
Chiltern Family and Mediation Centre
City of London Police
Civil and Public Service Association
Communication Workers Union
Concord Associates, London
Conflict Resolution Services, Stillorgan, Eire
Coventry and Warwickshire Family Mediation
Coventry Community Safety Mediation Service
Crutes, Solicitors, Carlisle
Cumbria Family Mediation Service
Derby Council for Voluntary Service
Derby Mediation Service
Derby Rape Crisis
Derbyshire Dales Victim Support
Devon Social Services
Edinburgh Community Mediation
Elder Mediation Project, London

Endeavour Training, London
Environment Council
Erewash Housing Department
FAME, Nottingham
Family Law Consortium, London
Family Mediators Association
Fife Community Mediation
Funeral Ombudsman Service
Gloucestershire Probation Service
Greater Manchester Probation Service
Guildford Community Mediation
Hackney Mediation Service
Hampshire Constabulary
Hampshire Social Services
Haringey Mediation Service
Hastings and St. Leonards Mediation
Health Service Ombudsman
Helen Nicholson
Highfield Junior School, Plymouth
Home Office Research and Planning Unit
Hope Project, Stourbridge
Hounslow Social Services
Housing Association Ombudsman
Howard League for Penal Reform
ICOREC, Manchester Metropolitan University
Impossible Theatre
INCORE, University of Ulster
Institute for the Study and Treatment of Delinquency (ISTD), King's College, London
Insurance Ombudsman Bureau
Interfaith Network, London
International Institute of Peace Studies and Global Philosophy, London
Jain Academy, London
Jan Shimmin
Kingston Friends Workshop
Lambeth Mediation
Lambourn Court Counselling
Leeds Community Mediation
Legal Ombudsman
Lichfield Council for Voluntary Service
London Borough of Hounslow, Housing
London Borough of Richmond, Housing
London Court of International Arbitration
Luton Mediation
Maidstone Mediation
Mansfield Mediation Service
Marvel Mediation Service, Wrexham
Mediation Dorset
Mediation Manchester
Mediation Mid-Wales
Mediation Sheffield

Mediation UK
Mediation West Cornwall
MEND, London
Metropolitan Police Service
Milton Keynes Youth Crime Reduction
Mole Valley Mediation
North-West Leicestershire CVS
National Coalition Building Institute (NCBI)
National Council for Voluntary
Organisations
National Family Mediation
National Police Training
National Union of Journalists
Neath Port Talbot Youth Justice Service
Network Housing Association, Leicester
New Forest Mediation
New Prospect Housing Association, Tyne
and Wear
Newham Conflict and Change
Nora Doherty and Associates, Leamington
North Derbyshire Family Mediation
Northamptonshire Social Services
Northamptonshire Police
Northamptonshire Diversion Unit, Kettering
Northern Devon Community Mediation
Norwich Friendly Mediation
Nottingham Probation Service
Occupational Pensions Advisory Service
Ombudsman for Estate Agents
Oxford Brooks University
PANDA, Preston
Paramount Housing Association, Newbury
Peace and Reconciliation Group, Derry
Penge Churches Housing Association
Pensions Ombudsman
Penta Housing, London
Pilgrim Housing Association, Guildford
Plus Training, Royston
Plymouth Mediation
Police Complaints Authority
Post Adoption Centre Mediation Service
Quaker Peace and Service
Redditch Friends Housing Association
Reepham Housing Trust
Relate, Boston
Relate, Chesterfield
Relate, Derby
Relate, Herefordshire
Relate, Lincoln
Relate, Norwich
Relate, Shrewsbury
Relate, Warwick
Rochdale Mediation Service
Rollit Farrell and Bladon, Solicitors, Hull
Rushcliffe Council for Voluntary Service
Sandwell Mediation

Sheffield Victim-Offender Mediation
Shepherds Bush Housing Association
Shropshire Association for Sheltered Housing
Sneinton/St. Anns Mediation, Nottingham
Solicitors Family Law Association
South-East London Family Mediation
South-West London Probation Service
South Yorkshire Police
St. Edmundsbury Area Mediation Service
Sussex Family Mediation Service
Swale Mediation
Tallaght Community Mediation, Dublin
Tenant Participatory Advisory Service, North
Wales
Thames Valley Poiice
The Bridge Consultancy, Basingstoke
The Leaveners/Leap Confronting Conflict
Thurrock Council for Voluntary Service
Tower Hamlets Mediation Service
Transport and General Workers Union
Transport Salaried Staff Association
UNISON, Nottingham
Universities Association of Continuing
Education
University of Aberdeen, Law Department
University of Bradford, Department of Peace
Studies
University of Hull, Law Department
University of Portsmouth, Social Services
Research and Information Unit
University of Sheffield, Centre for
Criminological and Legal Research
University of Ulster, Centre for the Study of
Conflict
University of Westminster, School of Law
Venture Housing Association, Liverpool
Victim Support, London
Voluntary Action, Barnsley
Voluntary Action, Leeds
Voluntary Action, Westminster
Waltham Forest Neighbourhood Mediation
Wandsworth Independent Mediation
Warwickshire Probation Service
Watford Mediation Sewice
West Kent Independent Mediation
West Lancashire Council for Voluntary
Service
West Mercia Constabulary
West Yorkshire Probation Service
Westfield Housing Association, Workington
Wirral Social Services
Wolverhampton Mediation
Women's Coalition, Derry
World Court Project
Worthing Mediation.

Select Bibliography

This selection includes books referred to in the text and included in the further reading lists at the end of chapters, and some others which are useful in themselves and which may lead, through their own bibliographies, to work in certain specialist areas. An exhaustive list of books on conflict resolution would, in fact, be very long and include many further texts, particularly American, which are not readily accessible in most British libraries.

Abdennur, A. (1987), *The Conflict Resolution System: Volunteerism, Violence and Beyond*, University of Ottawa Press

Access to Justice ('The Woolf Report'), 1996

Acland, A. F. (1990), *A Sudden Outbreak of Common Sense: Managing Conflict Through Mediation*, Hutchinson Business Books

Acland, A. F. (1995), *Resolving Disputes Without Going to Court*, Century Books: London

Ahier, B. (1986), *Conciliation, Divorce and the Probation Service*, Social Work Monographs: Norwich

Al-Wahab, I. (1979), *The Swedish Institution of Ombudsman*, LiberForlag: Stockholm

Amy, D. (1987), *The Politics of Environmental Mediation*

Augsburger, D. A. (1992), *Conflict Mediation Across Cultures: Pathways and Patterns*, Westminster/John Knox Press, Louisville, Kentucky

Bennett, T., Martin, G., Mercer, C. and Woollacott, J. (Eds.) (1981), *Culture, Ideology and Social Process*, Open University Press, Milton Keynes

Bercovitch, J. and Rubin J. L. (Eds.) (1992), *Mediation in International Relations: Multiple Approaches to Conflict Management*, Macmillan

Bevan, A. (1992), *Alternative Dispute Resolution: A Lawyer's Guide to Mediation and Other Forms of Dispute Resolution*, Sweet and Maxwell: London

Birkenshaw, P. (1995), *Grievances, Remedies and the State*, Sweet and Maxwell: London

Bisno, H. (1988), *Managing Conflict*, Sage: California

de Bono, E (1982), *Conflicts: A Better Way to Resolve Them*, Penguin: London

Bossy, J. (Ed.) (1983), *Disputes and Settlements: Law and Human Relations in the West*, Cambridge University Press

Braithwaite, J. (1989), *Crime, Shame and Reintegration*, Cambridge University Press

Burchill, F. (1992), *Labour Relations*, Macmillan: London

Bush, R. and Folger, J. (1994), *The Promise of Mediation*, Jossey-Bass: San Francisco

Carpenter, J. (1995), *Another Way: Positive Response to Contemporary Violence*, Oxford University Press

Central London County Court (1996), *Mediation Pilot Scheme*

Clutterbuck, R. (1978), *Kidnap and Ransom: The Response*, Faber and Faber: London

Clutterbuck, R. (1981), *Living With Terrorism*, Faber and Faber: London

Clutterbuck, R. (1987), *Kidnap, Hijack and Extortion*, MacMillan, London

Cohen, R. (1995), *Students Resolving Conflict*, Goodyear Books

Cohen, S. (1985), *Visions of Social Control*, Polity Press: Oxford

Constantio C., and Merchant C. S. (1996), *Designing Conflict Management Systems*, Jossey-Bass: New York

Coser, L. (1956), *The Functions of Social Conflict*, Routledge and Kegan Paul: London

Crawley, J. (1992), *Constructive Conflict Management: Managing to Make a Difference*, Nicholas Brealey: London

Crozier, B. (1974), *A Theory of Conflict*, Hamilton: London

Curle A. (1995), *Another Way: Positive Response to Contemporary Violence*, Jon Carpenter: Oxford

D'Ambremenil, P. (1997), *Mediation and Arbitration*, Medico-Legal Practitioner Series, Cavendish Publishing: London

Darby J. (1994), *What's Wrong with Conflict*, Centre for the Study of Conflict, University of Ulster

Davies, G. (1988), *Access to Agreement: A Consumer Study of Mediation in Family Disputes*, Open University Press: Milton Keynes

Davies, G. (1992), *Making Amends: Mediation and Reparation in Criminal Justice*, Routledge: London

Davis, W. and Fouracre, P. (Eds.) (1986), *Settlement of Disputes in Early Medieval Europe*, CUP

Deech, R., 'Divorced from Reality', *The Spectator*, 4 November, 1995

Deutsch, M. (1973), *The Resolution of Conflict: Constructive and Destructive Processes*, Yale University Press

Dignan J., Sorsby A. and Hibbert, J. (1996), *Neighbour Disputes: Comparing the Cost-effectiveness of Mediation and Alternative Approaches*, University of Sheffield

Dingwall, R., and Eekelaar, J. (1988), *Divorce Mediation and the Legal Process*, Oxford

Duke, J. (1976), *Conflict and Power in Social Life*, Brigham Young University Press: Utah

Ellickson, R. C. (1991), *Order with Law; How Neighbours Settle Disputes*, Harvard University Press

Elson, M. (1986), *Green Belts: Conflict Mediation in the Urban Fringe*, Heinemann: London

Engle Merry, S. and Milner, N (Eds.) (1993), *The Possibility of Popular Justice: A Case Study of Community Mediation in the United States*

Environmental Council, The (1995), *Beyond Compromise: Building Consensus in Environmental Planning and Decision Making*

Fatic, A. (1995), *Punishment and Restorative Crime-Handling*, Avebury, Aldershot

Fine, N., and Macbeth, F. (1990), *Playing With Fire: Training for the Creative Use of Conflict*

Fisher, R. and Ury, W. (1991), *Getting to Yes: Negotiation Agreement Without Giving In*, Century Business: London

Folberg, J. and Taylor, A. (1990), *Mediation: A Comprehensive Guide to Resolving Conflicts Without Litigation*, Jossey-Bass: San Francisco

Folger, J. P. and Jones, T. S. (Eds.) (1994), *New Directions in Mediation: Communication Research and Perspectives*, Sage: California

Foster, R. J. and Ury, W. (1978), *International Mediation: Ideas for Practitioners*, International Peace Academy: New York

Foucault, M. (1975), *Discipline and Punishment*, Penguin: London

Freeman, M. (Ed.) (1995), *Alternative Dispute Resolution*, New York University Press

Friedman, G. (1993), *A Guide of Divorce Mediation: How to Reach a Fair, Legal Settlement at a Fraction of the Cost*, Workman Publishing, N. Yorkshire

Freire, P. (1972), *The Pedagogy of the Oppressed*, Penguin: London

Giddens, A. (1971), *Capitalism and Modern Social Theory*, Cambridge University Press

Giddens, A. (1978), *Durkheim*, Fontana: London

Giddens, A. (1989), *Sociology*, Polity Press: Cambridge

Graham, C. (1991), *The Non-Classical Ombudsman*, University of Sheffield

Grillo, T. (1991), 'The Mediation Alternative: Process Dangers for Women', *Yale Law Journal*, Vol 100:6

Haddington, K., *Mediation Training Manual: Preliminary Draft*, Justice Institute of British Columbia, 1996

Hamilton, P. (1983), *Talcott Parsons*, Routledge and Kegan Paul: London

Haynes, J. and Haynes, G. (1989), *Mediating Divorce*, Jossey-Bass: San Francisco

Highfield Junior School Plymouth and Alderson, P. (Ed.) (1997), *Changing Our School: Promoting Positive Behaviour*, Highfield Junior School and Institute of Education, University of London

Hochschild, A. R. (1983), *The Managed Heart*, University of California Press

Hudson, J. and Galaway, B. (1978), *Offender Restitution in Theory and Action*, Lexington Books: Lexington, Mass.

Income Data Services (1996), *Industrial Relations and Collective Bargaining*, Institute of Personnel and Development: European Management Guide

Irving, H. and Benjamin, M. (1995), *Family Mediation: Contemporary Issues*, Sage: California

Johnson, R. A. (1993), *Negotiation in the Workplace: Negotiation Basics*, Sage: California

Joll, J. (1977), *Gramsci*, Fontana: London

Kagel, S. and Kelly, K. (1989), *The Anatomy of Mediation*

Kindler, H. S. (1988), *Managing Disagreement Constructively*, Kogan Page

Kingston Friends (1991), *Introduction to Mediation*, Kingston Friends Workshop Group

Kingston Friends and Kingston Polytechnic (1989), *Conflict Management in the Classroom*, Kingston Friends

Kingston Friends Workshop Groups (1990), *Ways and Means: An Approach to Problem Solving*

Kressel, K., Pruit, D. G. *et al* (1989), *Mediation Research: The Process and Effectiveness of Third Party Intervention*, Jossey-Bass: San Francisco

Lall, R (Ed.) (1985), *Multilateral Negotiation and Mediation: Instruments and Methods*, Pergamon Press: London

Lederach, J. P. (1995), *Preparing for Peace: Conflict Transformation Across Cultures*, Syracuse University Press

Lewis, L. (1994), *Curing Conflict*, Pitman: London

Liebmann, M. (Ed.) (1996), *Arts Approaches to Conflict*, Jessica Kingsley Publishers, London

Longer-Term Impact of Family Mediation, The (1996), University of Newcastle

Looking Into The Future: Mediation and the Ground for Divorce, Green Paper (1993), Lord Chancellor's Department, Cmnd. 2799

Lord Chancellor's Department (1995), *Resolving Disputes Without Going to Court*, HMSO

Lupton, C., Barnard, S. and Swall-Yarrington, M. (1995), *Family Planning? An Evaluation of the Family Group Conference Model*, University of Portsmouth Social Services Research and Information Unit

Mackie K. N. (Ed.) (1991), *A Handbook of Dispute Resolution: ADR in Action*, Routledge: London

Marshall, T. (1985), *Alternatives to Criminal Courts* Gower: Aldershot

Marshall, T. (1985), *Bringing People Together: Mediation and Reparation Projects in Great Britain*, Home Office: London

Matthews, R. (Ed.) (1988), *Informal Justice?*, Sage: California

Mediation: The Making and Remaking of Cooperative Relationships: An Evaluation of the Effectiveness of Comprehensive Mediation (1994), University of Newcastle

Mediation UK (1996), *Directory of Mediation and Conflict Resolution Services*, Mediation UK: Bristol

Mediation UK (1996), *Guide to Starting a Community Mediation Service*, Mediation UK: Bristol

Mediation UK (1996), *Training Manual in Community Mediation Skills*

Mediation UK (1994), *Victim and Offender Mediation Handbook*

Merry, S. E. (1990), *Getting Justice and Getting Even: Legal Consciousness Among Working Class Americans*, University of Chicago Press

Merry, S.E. and Milner, N. (1993), *The Possibility of Popular Justice: A Case Study of Community Mediation in the United States*, University of Michigan Press

Millward, N. (1994), *The New Industrial Relations?*, Policy Studies Institute

Moody, S. and Mckay, R. (1995), *Green's Guide to ADR in Scotland*, Edinburgh

Moore, C. W. (1986), *The Mediation Process: Practical Strategies for Resolving Conflict*, Jossey-Bass, San Francisco

Noone, M. (1996), *Mediation*, Cavendish Publishing: London

Parkin, F., (1992), *Durkheim*, Clarendon Press, Oxford

Parkins, L. (1986), *Conciliation in Separation and Divorce*, Croom Helm

Peak Park Joint Planning Board (1992), *Access to Open Country: A Balanced Approach, A Draft Strategy*, Bakewell:The Board

Powell, E. (1989), *Kingship, Law and Society: Criminal Justice in the Reign of Henry V*, Clarendon Press: Oxford

Raynor, P. (1988), *Probation As An Alternative to Custody*, Avebury: Aldershot

Raynor, P. (1993), *Social Work, Justice and Control*, 2nd edn., Whiting and Birch: London

de Reuck, A and Knight, J. (Eds.) (1966), *Conflict in Society*, Churchill: London

Roberts A., and Umbreit, M., 'Victim-offender Mediation: The English Experience', *Mediation*, Summer 1996, Vol. 12:3

Roberts, M. (1988), *Mediation in Family Disputes: A Guide to Practice*, Wildwood House: Aldershot

Roberts, S. (1989), *Learning to Listen*, Careers and Occupation Information Centre: Sheffield

Saaty T. L. and Alexander J. M. (1989), *Conflict Resolution*, Praeger: New York

Seneviratne, M (1994), *Ombudsmen in the Pubic Sector*, Open University Press

Sidaway, R., 'The Use of Consensus Building in Planning and Conflict Resolution: A Brief Introduction to Consensus Building and Mediation Techniques'. A paper prepared for a joint conference of the Countryside Recreation Network and the Landscape Research Group, 19-20 November 1996, Peterborough, CRN, Cardiff

185

Sidaway, R (1997), *Access Management by Local Consensus: Reducing Environment Impacts by Negotiation*

Simkin, W. E. (1971), *Mediation and the Dynamics of Collective Bargaining*

Smith, A. and Robinson, A. (1996), *Education for Mutual Understanding: The Initial Statutory Years*

Smith, C. G. (Ed.) (1971), *Conflict Resolution: Contributions of the Behavioural Sciences*, University of Notre Dame Press: Indiana

Social Trends, 25, 26 and 27 (1995, 1996 and 1997), HMSO

Stagner, R. (1956), *Psychology of Industrial Conflict*, Wiley: New York

Thomas, K., 'Conflict and Conflict Management', in Dunnette, M. (Ed.) (1975), *The Handbook of Industrial and Organisational Psychology*, Rand McNally: Chicago

Tillert, G. (1991), *Resolving Conflict: A Practical Approach*, Sydney University Press

Touval, S. and Zortman, W. I. (Eds.) (1984), *International Mediation in Theory and Practice*

Tyrrell J. and Farrell S. (1995), *Peer Mediation in Primary Schools*, Centre for the Study of Conflict: University of Ulster

Tyrrell, J. (1995), *The Quaker Peace Education Project 1988-1994; Developing Untried Strategies*

Umbreit, M. (1995), *Mediating Interpersonal Conflicts: A Pathway to Peace*, CPI Publishing, Minnesota

Umbreit, M. (1994), *Victim Meets Offender: The Impact of Restorative Justice and Mediation*, Monsey, New York: Criminal Justice Press

UNISON Policy and Research (1993), *Local Bargaining: A Guide for UNISON Negotiators*

Veljanovski, C. (Ed.) (1991), *Regulators and the Market: An Assessment of the Growth of Regulation in the UK*, Institute of Economic Affairs: London

Warner, S. (1992), *Making Amends: Justice for Victims and Offenders. An Evaluation of the SACRO Reparation and Mediation Project*, Avebury: Aldershot

Witty, C. (1980), *Mediation and Society: Conflict Management in Lebanon*, Academic Press: London

Woolf, Lord (1996): see *Access to Justice* ('The Woolf Report')

Wright, M. and Galaway, B. (Eds.) (1989), *Mediation and Criminal Justice: Victims, Offenders and Community*, Sage: London

Wright, M. (1982), *Victim and Offender Mediation*, Barnett Books: London

Wright, M. (1996), *Justice for Victims and Offenders: A Restorative Response to Crime*, edn. 2, Waterside Press: Winchester

Zartman, W. and Touval, S. (1985), 'International Mediation, Conflict Resolution and Power Politics', *Journal of Social Issues*, Vol 41: 2

Zehr, H. (1990), *Changing Lenses*, Croom Helm.

Index

188

📖 Justice for Victims and Offenders

Martin Wright

SECOND EDITION

As featured in *The Guardian*

An informative addition to the excellent Waterside Press series *Vista*

(1996) ISBN 1 872 870 35 X £16

📖 Introduction to the Family Proceedings Court

Elaine Laken
Chris Bazell and
Winston Gordon

Foreword by Sir Stephen Brown
President of the Family Division of the High Court

Produced under the auspices of the Justices' Clerks' Society

. . . Because of its clarity of information and its lucidity of language and explanation *Introduction to the Family Proceedings Court* is a very accessible handbook *The Magistrate*

(1997) ISBN 1 872 870 46 5 £12

📖 Criminal Justice and the Pursuit of Decency

Andrew Rutherford

By reminding us that, without 'good men and women' committed to humanising penal practice, criminal justice can so easily sink into apathy and pointless repression, Andrew Rutherford has sounded both a warning and a note of optimism *Sunday Telegraph*. (First reprint, 1994) ISBN 1 872 870 21 X £12

📖 Relational Justice: Repairing the Breach

Jonathan Burnside and Nicola Baker (Eds.)

Foreword by Lord Woolf

As featured in *The Guardian*. (1994) ISBN 1 872 870 22 8. £10

📖 I'm Still Standing

Bob Turney

By a dyslexic ex-prisoner who is now a probation officer and media luminary—and whose progress has featured in *Hansard*. A fascinating story *The Law*. A truly remarkable book *Prison Writing*. A gripping story . . . Brutally honest *The Manchester Justice*. (1997) ISBN 1 872 870 43 0 £12

Available from Waterside Press, Domum Road, Winchester, SO23 9NN. Telephone/fax 01962 855567. Direct mail prices quoted: Please add £1.50 per book p&p to a maximum of £6 (UK only: postage abroad charged at cost). Cheques should be made payable to 'Waterside Press'. Organizations can be invoiced for two or more books on request.

SC

Until They Are Seven

His Honour John Wroath

An absorbing account of the origins of women's rights vis-à-vis their property and children. A work of detection, following the reports, records and court proceedings of the time. A compelling read. A true story, which can be compared with a Victorian novel. Written by the former senior family judge for Hampshire and the Isle of Wight.

ISBN 1 872 870 57 0 £16

WATERSIDE PRESS RESEARCH SERIES: No. 2

The Waterside Press Research Series is intended as a resource for libraries, researchers and specialists who would like to obtain papers which are not generally available. By arrangement with the authors of a range of highly specialised materials we offer the facility to obtain copies of their work from us.

In the Interests of the Child: A Study of Mediation, Conflict and Implications for the Child will be of interest to anyone concerned with divorce mediation in so far as children are concerned, including:

- mediators
- trainers
- lawyers; and
- researchers

The ultimate aim of this research is to contribute to the development of mediation practice whether in relation to the implications for the child, parental conflict or mediators' interventions. The research can also be used as a training aid, or in support of further specialist study.

A copy of *In the Interests of the Child* by Nicholas Eadon, Family Court Welfare Officer, Suffolk is available in its original format, bound and at a price of £85 (plus £3.50 p&p).

60 4012187 9